ADVANCE PRAISE FOR
TBD—TO BE DETERMINED

"A must-read for leaders at all stages of their career and at every level. Brenda's business and personal experiences bring clarity to any leader faced with managing change. TBD provides timeless advice for uncertain times. Reynolds' unique blend of warmth, wisdom, and real-world examples makes this an easy read, with big impact."

CHERI PHYFER, PRESIDENT, CONSUMER BRANDS GROUP AT SHERWIN-WILLIAMS

"I loved this book! Brenda Reynolds creatively argues her hypothesis: in most lives, our reliance on "Plan A" is an illusion; consequently we had best craft a "Plan Be." She draws the reader into her conversational narrative through storytelling, self-reflection, and metaphor, abundantly sprinkled with humor and empathy. Relying on her academic training and her extensive professional experience, she paraphrases and enlivens salient concepts by classic organization development theorists—Argyris, Bridges, Oshry, and Seashore—making them accessible to a new generation of leaders."

RUTH WAGNER, EXECUTIVE-IN-RESIDENCE & DIRECTOR OF THE MASTER'S OF SCIENCE IN ORGANIZATION DEVELOPMENT PROGRAM AT AMERICAN UNIVERSITY, WASHINGTON, DC

"TBD is such a brilliant work. It is so easy to read and profound at the same time in its wisdom and application. TBD provides readers with great insight. Reynolds acts as a guide through the jungle of uncertainty and puts readers on the path *and* the unexpected joy of discovery. After the first reading, I am left with images of her stories and her personal insights, woven together with research and the advice of other leaders.

TBD is a gem that needs to get out into the world. I find myself quoting it and telling some of the stories from my favorite chapters. Reynolds' words and descriptions have a precision that focuses the

W9-CHX-329

energy directly to the heart, and not just to the mind of the reader. This is a birth gift and one that she shares with others so beautifully."

Dr. Michael Durst, psychologist, author, *Management by Responsibility and Napkin Notes on the Art of Living Responsibly*

"Over one's career it becomes clear the only thing constant in any organization and many other aspects of life is change. TBD reminds leaders how to approach organizational and life change with sensitivity, strategy, and sensibility. Brenda is a masterful story-teller with an uncanny ability to make complex concepts simple and applicable to the workplace…and life space! Whether you are in a corporate leadership position or dealing with struggles in your life, TBD is well worth reading."

Roger A. Oxendale, President, Covenant Ministries of Benevolence; Founding President Nemours Children's Hospital; Former CEO Children's Hospital of Pittsburgh

"*TBD—To Be Determined: Leading with Clarity and Confidence in Uncertain Times* serves to awaken you and disrupt your compliance. It forces you to decide—lead or be left behind. Reynolds shows readers the compelling truth: uncertain times don't equate to uncertain leaders. When change is inevitable, transformation is possible."

S. Renee Smith, Nationally Recognized Self-Esteem & Branding Expert, Coach, Speaker, Author of *Self Esteem for Dummies*

"As a 20-year Senior Advisor in one of the most change-laden industries in business, I found TBD spot-on, purposeful and revolutionary. Reynolds has managed to corral the slippery topic of corporate change and business transition in the most grounded and thoughtful way, and offers masterful solutions to those of us leaders who aim to be the best, most powerful versions of ourselves. Bravo!"

Megan A. McNealy, First Vice President, Merrill Lynch Global Wealth Management

"We all meet with the unexpected at some point in our personal and/ or professional lifetimes. Regardless of which universe it transpires, the effect is cataclysmic. Reynolds' ability to recognize and articulate the impact to our ego, pride, and sense of failure is spot on. Further, her innate sense of the journey we must take and the lessons we learn as part of recovery are nothing less than awakening. I recently faced an extraordinary and unexpected setback. TBD allowed me the luxury of hitting the pause button, to see my situation as an opportunity to achieve clarity, and more importantly to reassess my priorities. I came away with the ability to define what I was looking for in an organization, what I enjoyed most, what I most valued, and ultimately what aligned most closely with me personally and professionally. I made my way through the "fog" and now appreciate a new sense of clarity that I may have lost sight of previously."

JENNIFER HAMILTON, FORMER COO OF MARY BRIDGE CHILDREN'S
HOSPITAL AND HEALTH NETWORK

"We are in an age within which we too often refuse to listen to and empathize with each other, which makes us slow to shift views, grow and change our minds. *TBD* is a wonderful—accessible and practical—guide that not only sparks change and growth on a personal level, but helps support this change and development throughout the organization. It reads like a primer of organization development thought and best practice."

HILE RUTLEDGE, PRESIDENT, OKA (OTTO KROEGER ASSOCIATES),
CO-AUTHOR OF THE BEST-SELLER *TYPE TALK AT WORK, AND GENERATION TRANSLATION*; AUTHOR OF THE *MBTI® INTRODUCTION WORKBOOK,*
THE *EQ WORKBOOK, AND THE FOUR TEMPERAMENTS WORKBOOK*

"Times of change and uncertainty require us to manage stress and support resilience in ourselves and others. This book is an essential tool for anyone wanting to successfully navigate through transitions at home or in the workplace. It offers practical and creative tips for developing an effective mindset and for building self-encouragement, self-compassion, and the courage needed in times of transition and uncertainty."

JANE SHURE, PHD, LCSW, PSYCHOTHERAPIST, LEADERSHIP
CONSULTANT, AUTHOR, TEDX SPEAKER- *BOOST RESILIENCE: TAKE CHARGE OF THE INNER CRITIC* & INNER WORRIER

TBD

TO BE DETERMINED

TBD

TO BE DETERMINED

Leading
with Clarity
and
Confidence in
Uncertain
Times

**YOUR GUIDE TO MANAGING
BUSINESS CHANGE WITH EASE**

BRENDA KLINE REYNOLDS

TBD—To Be Determined
Leading with Clarity and Confidence in Uncertain Times

Published by Station Square Media ®
1204 Broadway, 4th Floor, New York, NY 10001

Editor: Diane O'Connell, Write to Sell Your Book ®
Cover Design: Laura Duffy
Interior Design: Steven Plummer
Post-production Management: Janet Spencer King
Printed in the United States of America for Worldwide Distribution

ISBN: 978-0-9992268-0-3

Electronic editions:
Mobi ISBN: 978-0-9992268-1-0
EPUB ISBN: 978-0-9992268-2-7
First Edition
[NOTE: Unless permission was granted, names and identifying characteristics of individuals mentioned have been changed to protect their privacy.]

DEDICATION

For my sons, Tyler and Jason, who are living proof that uncertain times can yield amazing results.

TABLE OF CONTENTS

INTRODUCTION

"If you want to make God laugh, tell him about your plans."
—WOODY ALLEN

D O YOU REMEMBER your first leadership role? Remember how excited you were about becoming a leader? And then you quickly realized what it entailed.

If you're like most leaders, you were promoted based on your technical competence or your proficiency in some area. That promotion to leader threw you into the deep end of managing people, with limited training in doing so. And then you had to figure out how to lead in the midst of constant organizational change.

The fact is, as a leader, you work in a complex space, full of responsibility. Now, throw in a big change such as a merger or acquisition—or even a minor one such as a new addition to the team—and the job gets even more complicated. Layer on the loneliness that can come with the leadership space, where you are expected to know what to do and how to lead others through uncertain times. Truthfully, you yourself feel uncertain much of the time. Even the information you need for your plans is highly filtered on its way up the hierarchical ladder to you. It can be confounding, overwhelming, and isolating.

As a leader, complexity, responsibility, change, and uncertainty come with the job. You are entrusted not only with the job you need to get done, but also with the people in your organization. And both the job and the people come with their own complications and uncertainties. And while that leadership space can be lonely, you aren't alone with these challenges. The question is, how do you find your way when the answer is To Be Determined (TBD)? Learning how "to be" in times when the answer is unclear may be the single most important leadership muscle you need to build. How you manage uncertainty not only affects you, but also sends a big ripple through your organization. So, it matters to you and to everyone who works with you, too.

I've seen this ripple effect in organizations and leaders I've worked with. I've built a career out of supporting organizations and leaders—both newly minted and seasoned—through their confusing *"now what?"* moments and into greater clarity. I've spent over twenty-five years consulting to hundreds of major corporations, nonprofits and organizations. As an organization development consultant, I'm trained as an expert in change, transitions, and transforming organizations, teams, and leaders. I've had the honor of helping bring a new children's hospital to life, of guiding school districts through major growth and change, of supporting government clients, and of working with a diverse array of client systems.

I've also walked into thousands of scenarios of crisis and dysfunction. That comes with this work as well. I've coached burdened executives, turned around cultures that were in a nose dive, and coached coworkers who detested each other, helping them learn to coexist. Truthfully, as a successful and trusted consultant, I have no fear. I wade into confusion, dysfunction, outrage, and distrust. It's part of my job. It's part of forging new possibilities for my clients. And I'd like to help you find that same confidence during your complex times.

When change and confusion hit, our tendency is to get determined to get it behind us, right? To check that box. But the next change and the next round of uncertainty lurks just around the corner. So, our challenge is to figure out how "to be" during times of uncertainty again and again. ***TBD*** is my way of equipping you with the same tools I've used in my own career and as a consultant. They will help you to find clarity in the midst of uncertain times—whether it's a reorganization, a merger, a change in leadership, or any of the myriad of changes that can thrust you into a *"now what?"* moment. You will use this information over and over. And doing so will build this muscle, grow your confidence, and help you stand out among other leaders. Ideally, it will become part of your leadership DNA. You, your team, and your organization will all benefit.

BE READY FOR PLAN "BE"— PLAN A IS AN ILLUSION

I haven't always been a consultant. I have firsthand experience leading and dealing with change. I've held corporate leadership roles, and I even spent the first four years of my career as a teacher. Dealing with hormonal eighth and ninth graders was a bit crazy at times and kept me on my toes. But corporate life was equally unpredictable.

1993 was one of those unpredictable years. I was working for an environmental consulting firm as their manager of training and development. I was proud of the impact the team and I had made on the company and its culture. We had done damage control from my predecessor, forged trusting relationships at all levels of the organization, and created a training network of individuals from across our forty regional offices, which was showing great promise for future headway.

That year, I had the opportunity and responsibility of planning the organization's Corporate Annual Meeting. This was a big event that the organization made a very serious financial investment in, and senior leaders looked forward to attending it in Philadelphia. So, I worked feverishly day in and day out at the conference room table, constructing a meeting that no one would forget. I crossed my t's and dotted my i's, determined to create the perfect event—*perfection* and *planning* being concepts my twenty-something self still believed in. After all, this event was big, and I was going to be very visible to the top five hundred leaders from our organization.

I was also very big and quite visible, literally. My beach ball belly stood between me and the paper plans on the conference room table. As I cooked up this meeting, my body cooked up my first son. I glanced at the project planning calendar on the wall, noting two key dates: the February meeting and my April due date. I pulled the company org chart closer in front of me. It still had the line drawn on it from my new boss—the underqualified one who was friends with the president, needed a job, and had recently landed in my otherwise upward-moving career trajectory. That line on the org chart was a constant reminder of our first meeting.

"So, you work closely with everyone in the organization?" she asked.

"Yes," I replied, proud of the progress and partnerships I'd forged over the three years prior, despite a challenging start.

"I see," she responded, much less enthusiastically than I had felt. "Even the Executive Team?" she queried, while dangling a red marker over the org chart on the desk between us.

"Yes." I smiled. I waited for her positive acknowledgment that she was walking into an environment of trust with our internal clients, and that we had established credibility at every level of the organization.

Instead, the red marker landed. It drew a thick horizontal line separating the top half from the bottom half of the boxes on the org chart.

"See this line? You no longer interact with anyone above it. I do."

I met her eyes in stunned silence, knowing the expected reaction was quiet acceptance.

And then I got more determined than I had ever been in my career. I needed to change her mind. Perhaps this well-planned and well-executed corporate meeting would have her rethink that red line.

But days before the big meeting, my beach ball belly got in the way again. I found myself lying in the Chester County Hospital. While chatting with a nurse about this false alarm that had sent us rushing to the hospital for a baby checkup and some monitoring, a different type of boss graced the doorway—the doctor. He came ready to draw lines, too.

"You'll be on bed rest for the next few weeks," he declared.

"But that just can't be. I have a big corporate meeting to oversee at work in a few days!"

He looked at me with the same authority I had seen in my boss's eyes the day of the line drawing. "Well, you might want to call them now to explain that you won't be there."

I met his eyes in stunned silence, again knowing the only possible reaction was quiet acceptance. Another line had been drawn in my career, and I didn't like it one bit.

Months later, I found myself as a new mom approaching my return to work. Ironically, my boss had called me routinely to implore me to come back. Surprisingly, she'd agreed to an arrangement for me to return on a part-time basis, while keeping my leadership responsibilities. That offer seemed too good to be true.

Turns out it was. Upon my return, my boss announced she had changed her mind. Feeling blindsided, I found myself reporting to a colleague whom I had hired and trained. This colleague had been doing my job while I was on leave. Looking back, my boss's ultimate decision made some sense, but it certainly wasn't handled well. The sudden switch took me by surprise and equally stunned my colleague and staff. I was left wondering what happened and *now what*? But I swallowed hard and once again accepted the reality, as unreal as it was.

I poured myself into my project work while beginning to set the stage for a consulting practice of my own. After landing my first client, I provided a four-month notice out of respect for the team and the department, intending to see the project I was currently working on to its conclusion. Instead, my line-drawing boss questioned this advance notice with suspicion and asked for my two-week notice. I obliged. Ironically, months later, she called me back to consult for them as BKR Consulting.

Now, here's the thing. Three sets of plans had to implode for my consulting career to emerge. Three!

I learned early on that plan A is an illusion. Not that there's anything wrong with planning. We simply can't expect things to go exactly as planned. Expect plan B. Also expect all sorts of emotions to get stirred up. I can tell you that getting this new boss, being limited in my interactions with key people in the organization, being put on bed rest, missing that big corporate meeting, and then returning to work under completely unexpected conditions stirred up a whole host of emotions—shock, disappointment, surprise, fear, and anger, to name a few.

Perhaps you've picked up this book because of a plan A that just hasn't worked out. Take comfort that an imploding plan A is often leading to an even better outcome. But it doesn't feel good at the time, and we can't necessarily see the benefit. Nor does it feel like a benefit.

If some plan B has you reacting emotionally right now, let's begin by normalizing it—because you are not only working through the change, but also the emotions that come with it. Dealing with plan B and the accompanying emotions is a package deal. That's why I call it plan "be." We need to figure out how *to be* with the change and the emotion it stirs up. Understanding this process will be key for leading yourself and others through uncertain times.

HOW TO USE THIS BOOK

It isn't enough to read this book. Knowing something and doing something with what you know are two different things. I want you to begin *applying* what you read to your situation immediately. To guide you in that process, I've added what I'm calling "clarity boxes" throughout each chapter. They are a place to pause, think about the changes you are managing, and make notes to help shed some light on your situation. If you commit to answering these questions, you will be well on your way to some clarity, beginning with chapter one.

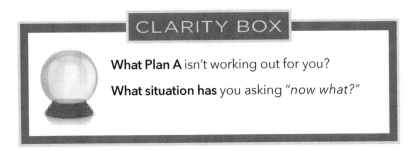

CLARITY BOX

What Plan A isn't working out for you?

What situation has you asking *"now what?"*

This book is organized into ten chapters, each highlighting a principle that can equip you to navigate change and uncertain times. Each chapter is based on a key theory, experience, concept, or tool and is illustrated by examples from my consulting and personal experiences. Through stories, case studies, and clear, practical teaching, I aim to shed light on how to best navigate uncertainty by learning how *to be* with it. Each chapter ends with a summary of reminders for mastering plan "be" since we've established that plan A is an illusion.

I have witnessed clients achieve great comfort and success by applying some of this classic information to their situations. And that's what I want you to find in these pages: some clarity, some comfort, and some help in getting to the other side of whatever new or uncertain situation you find yourself managing.

Certain lessons may feel like comforting confirmation of practices you already have in place. Others may be reminders, new thinking, or ideas that really stretch you.

Each chapter reveals a way of being in these complex and uncertain times. You'll find advice and strategies that, when put into practice, will bring you to the other side confidently. They will pave the way to some surprising and welcome clarity.

Like you, I'm constantly learning and being reminded about how to lean into uncertainty. In fact, I was reminded yet again while trying to figure out a title for this book.

I had no idea what to call it. I didn't like the not knowing. I found myself growing increasingly determined to land on a title. But the more determined I got, the more elusive it got. It wasn't until I let go and shared with colleagues that the title of the book was "still to be determined" that it became clear.

That was the title. *TBD. To Be Determined*. After all, managing uncertain times of change requires those two ingredients—*determination* and an ability *to be* with uncertainty. As a leader, I'm going to assume you have the determination part mastered. That can be the easier part. This book helps with the difficult task of figuring out how *to be* with the uncertainty for a while, knowing that clarity will eventually come.

If I've done this right, you'll learn how *to be* with whatever uncertainty you are facing as a leader.

What you actually get out of it, though, is TBD. So, turn the page. No sense going it alone.

CHAPTER 1

BE READY TO PLAN THE CHANGE...AND PLAN TO TRANSITION

"Change is great. You go first."
—MAC ANDERSON AND TOM FELTENSTEIN

WOULD IT SHOCK you to know that up to 70 percent of all change initiatives fail? Research carried out by Pat Zigarmi and Judd Hoekstra at The Ken Blanchard Companies in 2010[1] revealed this shocking fact, suggesting that most change initiatives are doomed to failure from the start. Why is that? After all, leaders and organizations are typically good at strategizing for change. Time and resources are dedicated to studying what needs to change, mapping out what needs to be done, setting milestones, budgeting for the change, and creating a project plan. Project managers and change experts get engaged in the process. The *what we need to DO* is crafted into a change management plan for implementation. The tactics and measures of success are identified. Good thinking and logic are applied.

So, what gets in the way?

Even with excellent planning, there's one thing that often trips us up. It's the reason so many change efforts fail.

Emotions! Both ours and others'. Perhaps you've been trained to believe there's no place for emotions in the workplace, but rest assured, they show up. The thing is, they are so often underestimated or just not factored in. And they can't be neatly mapped out on a project plan. They're messy. They often aren't accounted for during change, yet they are a major factor in moving through change successfully or failing miserably.

Don't take my word for it. In 1985, the beverage powerhouse, Coke, made a decision in the US market that threatened the entire global brand. Coke was losing market share to archrival Pepsi. And they made a big play to introduce a new formula that had been test-marketed. They rolled it out with great fanfare.

But "New Coke" was an epic fail. And only seventy-nine days after abandoning the ninety-nine-year-old formula created by Dr. John Pemberton, the old Coke was resurrected as "Coca-Cola Classic." "New Coke" was demoted to "Coke II" in 1992 and then killed off over the next decade.

Turns out the public had some pretty strong feelings about relegating the original Coke that they knew to the archives of history. The company failed to take the customer's feelings and loyalty to the brand into account, creating serious consequences.

Yes, every *change* effort also includes an emotional *transition*. So, let's make a necessary distinction between a change and a transition.

THE DIFFERENCE BETWEEN CHANGE AND TRANSITION[*]

What is change? You might think that would be an easy question to answer, but most people use the term too broadly. William Bridges, author, speaker, and organizational consultant, says there are actually two components to our experience—there is the *change*, but there is

---

[*] 2. The conceptual framework underlying this chapter is based on the work of William Bridges with Susan Bridges. See especially *Managing Transitions*, Da Capo Lifelong Books, Philadelphia Press, 2017.

also the *transition*. In his classic books, *Transitions* and *Managing Transitions*, he differentiates between the two.[2]

Change is defined as the *external event* that is happening to you.

The change could be something you've chosen or something imposed on you. It could be a positive change (a promotion, a relocation to a desirable city) or a negative change (a job loss, a necessary move from your dream home to more affordable housing). Either way, there are concrete steps in the change process that you can map out.

Let's use the moving example. If you're a leader, it's likely you've had to move yourself and your family more than once. Or perhaps you've had to lead your team through an office space move. During a personal move, you know you'll need to get the house ready to be put on the market, hire a realtor, sell your current home, pack up, buy a new home, and unpack. These are tangible steps you will take to get you from house A to house B.

When you relocate your office space, there's a clear plan in place for packing up and moving everything from your office belongings to the computers. It looks quite doable as you note all of the actions and milestones on paper. It's what you know needs to happen. There are concrete, logical steps that you can plan for. What isn't taken into account here is how messy living this change can be. And I don't *just* mean all the boxes and clutter. That's because it's not only a change, but a *transition*.

What is a transition? Bridges defines the transition as the psychological component of the change. It can best be represented by the tissues everyone uses as they pack boxes and say goodbye to their current home and its memories or the coworkers they've shared space with for years. The *transition* is the human and emotional component that accompanies the change. It's the psychological journey that we often underestimate. I see leaders and organizations make this mistake time after time. Either they forget to consider the emotional transitions that a change in the workplace will trigger, or they assume it's not their job to worry about feelings.

Yet, even when a change is something you've chosen and is moving you in a positive direction, the emotional component is like a fog that rolls in over your nice, neat project plan. While you are excited about moving into your dream home, your children may be less than thrilled to leave their current school. While you've worked hard to lobby for better office space for your team, they may seem focused on what they'll be giving up from the old space. The uncertainty of that new location or new neighborhood stirs up emotions. Everyone seems melancholy in the midst of this positive change and much less excited than you'd expect.

If the emotional part of the change, *the psychological transition* of those affected, is glossed over, this change may not go as smoothly as it could—either for you or for others impacted by the change. The adjustment takes time.

During times of change, it's often the transition that trips us all up. As a leader, understanding the psychological journey can help you and your colleagues move through change with your eyes wide open. To understand what's going on with those experiencing the *change*, you can ask, "What do you *think* about this change?" But to understand where they are with the *transition* requires you to ask, "How are you *feeling* about this change?" You'll be surprised at how much more you learn. It's worth reflecting on both questions—for yourself, too.

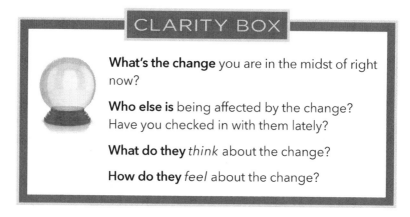

CLARITY BOX

What's the change you are in the midst of right now?

Who else is being affected by the change? Have you checked in with them lately?

What do they *think* about the change?

How do they *feel* about the change?

DEAL WITH EMOTIONS DURING CHANGE OR YOU'LL BE DEALING WITH RESISTANCE

Appreciating that emotions about a change are normal can help us to be kinder and gentler with ourselves and others. And it can help us to be more strategic when planning how to roll out change in the workplace.

In the business world, when the emotional impact of change on the people affected in the organization isn't accounted for, important changes are stopped dead in their tracks. I've witnessed a service organization identify the two most important business units in their system and pour hundreds of thousands of dollars into improving their operations, practices, and procedures in an effort to create a better customer experience. The employees, however, felt the changes were being imposed and that their input and feelings about the changes had been largely disregarded.

Years later, very little had really changed because the staff had resisted the new ways. However, there was one big result: both the leaders and the employees were frustrated, and additional dollars needed to be spent to deal with the problems that the resistance created.

The impact of feelings about change can be like radon, that invisible gas that seeps into the foundation of our homes. We don't think about it until there's a problem. It's the threat we don't see. I've seen many leaders forge ahead with changes, but when they turn around, no one seems to be following them.

I've witnessed continuous improvement efforts in organizations go south because of this. The concept of continuous improvement is hardly something we can argue with. I mean, who doesn't see the benefit of thinking about how things could be better, right? Perhaps your organization follows a formal process for doing this. You bring teams of people together, usually those with the best understanding of the process or situation you want to improve upon. The team looks at how things are currently being done. They chart the steps in the process, how long each step takes, and other data points. They then brainstorm possible improvements. Ultimately, some new ways of operating emerge—new ways that are worthy of experimentation for the benefits they may yield to customers, employees, and performance.

However, standing between these new and improved procedures and the results is one thing: the people who weren't in the room. People with feelings about these changes, who simply don't want to move away from their comfortable old practices. Humans who detest change in the same way I hated the change that the thick red line on the org chart represented in my work life. Our inner two-year-old—the one who can pitch a major fit in the grocery store, shrieking, throwing itself on the floor, body stiff and daring a parent to figure out how to deal with it—comes to life.

We create a great plan and make significant investments for important changes that make meaningful and logical sense, and nobody complies. They all resist. But it isn't only employees who resist. We all do. I confess to being guilty of this as a leader. In 1991, one of my direct reports, John, was attending conferences and then squirreling himself away in his office to work on learning more about this thing he claimed would change the world. I was so frustrated that I began to question his performance. He appeared to be playing instead of working. So, I limited the time he could allot to that work and began to do a bit of micromanaging. Turns out John *was* playing—with a little thing called the World Wide Web. I look back at that now and am chagrined. But my own resistance was alive. Like many, I was resisting what I didn't understand. I couldn't grasp this new technology and its alleged impact. And I couldn't feel on board with a change I didn't understand. I realize now that John had every right to see me as the one standing in the way of his attempt at forging progress in our department and organization.

WHY THIS RESISTANCE TO CHANGE?

Changes big or small can raise resistance because they create an unsettledness in us. Let's be honest. How many of us have held on to a job we've stopped feeling passionate about just because it was safe and comfortable? Or a relationship that's long past its shelf life?

Why do we rebel against changes—even those we think could be good for us? In part, because we like the familiar. We like things to be easy. We don't want to mark the ending of a familiar way of doing things. It's nice to go on auto-control and not have to think so much. It's called unconscious competence. We don't want to stop doing what's become comfortable in order to learn something new and foreign. Changes and plan B's swing us into a state called conscious incompetence[3] where we don't feel confident in our situation, where we have to really think about what we're doing.

The best example I can remember of this is learning to drive. I learned to drive an automatic transmission car when I turned sixteen. So, I knew how to drive. But as a senior in college, I fell in love with a God-awful, rust-colored, unsexy Chevy Chevette that I just had to have. In fact, I loved it so much I decided to buy it—despite the fact that it was a manual transmission, and I had no clue how to drive it. My dad had the unfortunate honor of being with me and in the passenger seat when we drove it home from the dealership. I was so proud . . . and equally clueless. Once I got us going (an accomplishment in and of itself), we hit a red light. What did I do?

Accelerate! My dad braced himself while screaming, "Why didn't you stop?!!" To which I had an obvious and sensible answer: "I didn't know how. I just got us going."

When life or work hands us plan B, we can be like that, too. We are moving along, easy breezy, and really don't want to have to stop, learn something new, process feelings, acknowledge some ending, and begin again. A new way of doing something represents the end of unconscious and easy action. And we mourn it, rebel against it like that red light, and keep doing what we know, moving along as we have been. Learning to drive that manual transmission car was hard. I had to think about my feet, the brake, the clutch, the gears. I couldn't imagine I'd ever get this new driving process down. I remember thinking I'd never again be able to drive through McDonald's and eat a burger. Dealing with a burger and a gearshift seemed impossible. Yet, in time, I did manage to do both. But it took time.

I didn't exactly plan too well when it came to learning to drive a stick shift. So, do better than I did. Plan your change. Or, if you are hit with an unexpected change, start to formulate a plan. Begin to think about what's next. Go ahead. Create your timeline, actions, and deadlines. That's important. But while you're at it, realize that emotions will get stirred up that can't neatly be placed on any timeline. Some changes are emotional walks in the park. The transition is easy. Others may take years. There's no way of predicting how long it will take to "be on board with the new change" or "get over things." But if we understand the stages of emotional transition, we can give ourselves and others grace in the process and ensure that we don't get stuck.

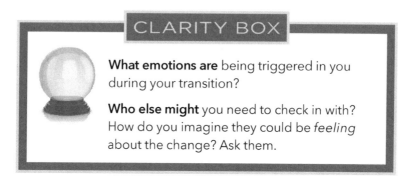

CLARITY BOX

What emotions are being triggered in you during your transition?

Who else might you need to check in with? How do you imagine they could be *feeling* about the change? Ask them.

UNDERSTANDING THE JOURNEY FROM "WHAT WAS" TO "WHAT WILL BE"

Think about moving through change as an emotional journey with three phases to it. We move back and forth between these phases on our way to fully accepting change. Bridges refers to those stages as endings, the neutral zone, and new beginnings. I think of them as a journey from *what was* to *what will be* with a lot of *uncertainty* in between.

Understanding more about these phases will help you to avoid some common pitfalls.

WHAT WAS

1. This is the letting go stage. Every emotional transition begins this way. It's unavoidable and necessary.

When plan A falls through, we don't typically dust ourselves off, casually utter, "Oh well," and move into plan B. We need some time to let go of *what was* before we can ever begin to move along toward *what will be*. Letting go of what was is our first order of emotional business.

Consider this extreme example to illustrate my point. You are at a funeral. You are in line to talk with the grieving widow. As you draw near, you hug her, lean in, and whisper, "Well, I guess that's over. After all, death is inevitable. Time to move on. Have I got the guy for you!"

If you gasped, there's hope for you. This poor widow needs time to grieve, move through a psychological transition, and then consider *what will be*. We all do. We need time to come to terms with what we've lost.

2. All change is experienced first as a loss—even when the change will be a good one.

We mourn the loss of what was comfortable and known. We're thrilled for the promotion, but miss parts of our old job. We're happy about our expanded role, but miss our old team. We love our new space, but miss the restaurants that were once in walking distance for lunch. On the home front, we're excited about launching a child to college, but having them move out is a bittersweet adjustment. We often mark changes with rituals of letting go. If a leader is retiring or moving on, there's often an event that acknowledges him or her, honors what he/she contributed, and invites others to speak about those times. When families move, there's often a going away party where pictures are taken of the house and friends being left behind. Rituals help us to mark endings so that we have a chance to process our feelings about them.

3. It takes time to move past the emotions of the *what was* stage. How long it takes is dependent on the magnitude of the change and each individual.

As we adapt to any new change—good or bad, chosen or imposed—feelings about what's ending hit us first. Even when I sold that rust-colored Chevette years later, upgrading to a sporty RX7, I still felt a twinge of emotion watching it drive away. I couldn't help but think about learning to drive it, Dad's face when I ran that red light, and the great college road trips I'd had in that car. I needed to do some emotional letting go. Now, in this case, I could do so quickly and move on. Other situations require much more letting go time.

One of the toughest changes I've observed occurs in small entrepreneurial organizations. As they grow, they move from being casual and informal in the way they conduct business to needing to formalize practices. This cultural shift stirs up a lot of emotion. Some people let go easily; others really cling to the way things have been and take much longer in letting go. So, we need to give ourselves and others the grace to do so.

4. Focusing on *what will be* is not a shortcut for mourning *what was*. Avoid the cheerleader tendency.

A common mistake that we often make is trying to psych ourselves or others up about a change. We fall into the trap of focusing on the *what will be*, thinking we can skip right to it. "You're gonna love it!" we exclaim. "It's going to be so much better. It's going to make your work so much easier." We oversell the future state. Remember the last technology upgrade your organization heralded as the next best thing since sliced bread, which guaranteed to bring great efficiencies with it? But often no one's listening because they're focused on what they're giving up. They need to do some mourning about what's going to be different and what they're giving up that was nice and familiar. We think the louder we speak or the more excited we are, the more likely we are to garner support. Meanwhile, the staff only hears Charlie Brown's teacher's voice in their heads: "Wah, wah, wah."

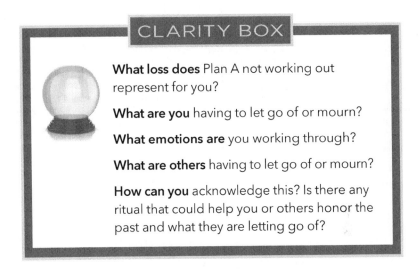

CLARITY BOX

What loss does Plan A not working out represent for you?

What are you having to let go of or mourn?

What emotions are you working through?

What are others having to let go of or mourn?

How can you acknowledge this? Is there any ritual that could help you or others honor the past and what they are letting go of?

UNCERTAINTY

Acknowledging and giving ourselves time to work through *what was* will keep us from getting stuck in the past and keep us moving. In time, the emotions of letting go will fade.

But as we're letting go of *what was* and preparing for *what will be*, we find ourselves in limbo. The big question is "now what?" Our feet feel firmly planted in midair. Welcome to uncertainty.

Because even when a change happens quickly, the adjustment may not. Uncertainty is that in-between space.

During a move, there's a time when your old house is ripped apart while you're packing. A nice, orderly new space has yet to appear.

As a new hire starting a new job, you sit through your new hire orientation. You're no longer in your old job, but you aren't squarely in your new job yet.

If you're in the midst of a divorce, your old life as you knew it is gone, but the new one isn't in view.

In the workplace, one leader retires and a new one has just arrived. It isn't the way it was any more, but it's not the way it's going to be just yet. Incoming new leaders are smart to use those early months to get to know the new team members, learn about the organization, ask questions, and learn from the past—before forging a plan for some bright, new, shiny future that activates the tantrum-inclined two-year-old in their direct reports. Until the staff move through this psychological transition, they can't fully move forward to embrace the change or the new leader.

There are two key things to remember about the uncertainty stage:

1. There are no detours around uncertainty. We must move through it. And it takes time.

This stage can be unsettling. We like things to feel definite. We want to be on the other side of whatever change we're experiencing, once and for all. But this stage has more question marks associated with it than periods. Our temptation is to try to take some shortcut through the uncertainty. But there isn't one. We're tempted to rush through it to settle the butterflies in our stomach or the anxiety we're experiencing. TBD is meant to help you make the most of being in this state.

2. We need to see the good in this stage.

That's right. The good in this space of uncertainty.

Let's use a job loss to illustrate what I mean. Perhaps you or someone you know has had this experience. A job loss is traumatic. Some people can't bear the uncertainty of being between jobs, so they take the first job offer that comes their way. Others use that time between jobs to reevaluate. They think about who they are in this stage of their lives, what they really want, and what's important to them. They consider career shifts. These are the people who ultimately say it was the best thing that ever happened to them. Now, that's not to say that hanging out in uncertainty was easy or fun. It's not to minimize the emotions they experienced and the discomfort of the uncertainty they faced when they lost their jobs. And they may not want to go through it again anytime soon, but they took full advantage of the *uncertainty* space.

Whether it's job losses, relationship breakups, company mergers, or health challenges, the uncertainty space affords us some opportunity. It's a chance to reflect, consider possibilities, explore creative options, and make choices before locking in a new reality. It's a space for coming into our potential. To quote Jack Canfield, author of *The Success Principles*, "If you are not a little bit uncomfortable every day, you're not growing. All the good stuff is just outside your comfort zone."

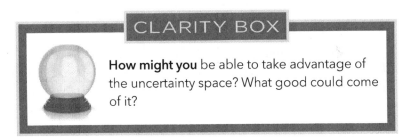

CLARITY BOX

How might you be able to take advantage of the uncertainty space? What good could come of it?

CAUTIONS ON THE WAY TO "WHAT WILL BE"

The speed of the change doesn't necessarily correlate to the time it takes for our emotional transition.

The change can happen quickly, but the emotional adjustment may take time.

As a leader, you're likely to be farther down the road with the adjustment than others are. Practice patience.

Whether you are a leader or a parent, you may know about a change long before others are informed of it. You've had a head start in adjusting to the change and processing your emotions. Upon announcing the change, you may expect your staff or family to be synced up with you. But they can't be. They'll lag behind for a while. They need time to let go and mourn the *what was* first.

You're ready to roll and eager for *what will be*. They're digging their heels in, mourning, or playing out some emotional drama over what they need to let go of. You'll need to remember this and be patient.

It's like this. Imagine you are watching a football game on your DVR. Your team members are watching the same game on DVR in the room next to you, but you're slightly ahead of them in the action. You're watching the third quarter where your team recovers from a big fumble and goes on to score a touchdown. But your team members are a minute behind you, watching that fumble and unsure of what will happen next. Even that twenty-second delay has you feeling very different things. So, as the leader, you may need to put down your pom-poms and practice some patience until your teammates catch up.

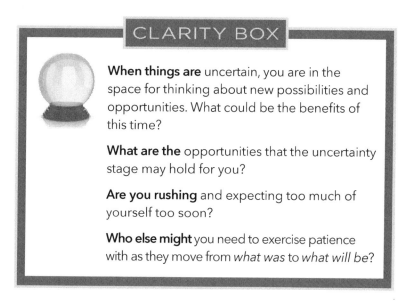

CLARITY BOX

When things are uncertain, you are in the space for thinking about new possibilities and opportunities. What could be the benefits of this time?

What are the opportunities that the uncertainty stage may hold for you?

Are you rushing and expecting too much of yourself too soon?

Who else might you need to exercise patience with as they move from *what was* to *what will be*?

"WHAT WILL BE"

On the other side of *what was* and *uncertainty* is a new reality—your *what will be* shows up. It's the easy part of the metamorphosis.

Maya Angelou, author and civil rights activist, put it best: "We delight in the beauty of the butterfly, but rarely admit the changes it has gone through to achieve that beauty."

Whatever has you reaching for this book may feel challenging. I get it. But you will emerge from that soupy cocoon eventually. Your new situation will have benefited from that time in the cocoon where you incubated on what was possible, explored options and possibilities, and generated creative solutions. The more consciously you lead yourself and others through the uncertainty—both the changes you need to plan for and the emotional transition that will accompany it—the better you'll be when the new reality shows up. In fact, the new reality is easy to adopt if we take full advantage of the uncertainty stage and don't get stuck or derailed by it. We need to see it as a normal stage of the change process.

Consider uncertainty a good friend that doesn't let us get complacent. It nudges us out of accepting "good enough" to move into "even better." It forces us to explore *now what?* With a lot of changes in my rearview mirror—a divorce and a new start in my professional life—I asked myself, *"Now what?"* And I began writing again and acting on lifelong dreams I had left by the wayside. The *what will be* part of the process can be downright exciting when you land in it.

FROM UNCERTAINTY TO TRANSFORMATION

When big change hits organizations, it often affects hundreds and thousands of people. One change can be like a falling domino that sets off a chain reaction. Those changes can feel like a crisis. But managed consciously, those changes can result in a transformation.

A good friend of mine is a high-ranking executive in a Fortune 100 company. His name has been changed to protect even the wonderful, so I'm going to call him Kevin. His story is a reminder to expect the unexpected—in his case, a merger—and get busy with leading through the transition.

Kevin had been working at this company for quite a while when it merged with a much larger company in the same industry. At the time, he was a year and a half into a "big break" opportunity, managing 150 people in several locations.

Because of the merger, all the functions Kevin was managing would be moved into the larger company's operations. So, everyone working for him would be out of a job in the next twelve to eighteen months. So much for plan A! It was plan B time. What a huge challenge for him and for his whole team. They were all pretty young, and so there were big concerns around both continuity of service and retention of talent.

"At the outset, things looked pretty bleak and dismal," said Kevin.

But, as Kevin put it, "Adversity brought out the best in the team." In a situation that could easily have led to backstabbing and sabotage and hostility, his team was open and honest with each other. Instead of hiding information, they shared it as soon as they could. Instead of making secret deals and blindsiding team members, they talked candidly about what was going on. During this uncertain time, they explored what was possible. Kevin engaged those being impacted during the change, and they openly discussed how the transition was feeling. Many leaders wait until they have all the answers before communicating. But that's not necessary. An honest "we don't know yet" goes a long way to building trust. There's just no such thing as over-communicating during times of major change and transition.

The result of open and honest communication during this uncertain time? "We nailed this thing," Kevin said.

They pulled off seamless service delivery, fulfilling all of the team's obligations to the company without skipping a beat. On top of that, they managed smooth career reassignments for pretty much everyone on the team—moving them to different roles within the merged company. Very few were forced out who didn't want to leave.

"It was really satisfying to do right by people in the organization," said Kevin. "All these years later, I still know many of the folks who were impacted. Lots of them are still here, and it's been rewarding to see their growth."

This success also helped Kevin make a name for himself in the merged entity, which led to lots of new opportunities for him.

This could be a simple lesson about the value of open communication during times of change as a way of helping others through their emotional transition. Open and ongoing communication is so often underrated as a powerful tool of leadership. And as important as that is, there's a bit more to the story.

For Kevin, underneath it all was his desire to be genuine, to care about his company, and to take pride in how the people who work for him feel about working there.

"Too many things in corporate America are fake," Kevin said. "For too many people, their best skill is acting. If you can be genuine, everything can be so much easier. I was born with a certain amount of empathy. So, I get more out of people by valuing them and creating the right environment."

As Kevin's situation demonstrates, if the *what was* and *uncertainty* phases of transition are well managed, the new state of *what will be* takes care of itself.

Don't get me wrong, your team members may not be dancing in the streets about the impending changes, but they also won't be pitching a fit on the cafeteria floor. Be a leader who considers the emotions that go along with the change. Managing the transition through the mourning of *what was*, through the desert of *uncertainty*, and into the new reality adeptly is a skill that gets leaders promoted. And Kevin was promoted.

Managing transitions well keeps you in the driver's seat, even when the circumstances around you don't seem controllable. It doesn't mean the red lights on your commute will go away. Like change, they are inevitable. But it may mean that you learn to shift gears more adeptly between *what was* and *what will be*. No more fear of red lights. Instead, an appreciation for the yellow lights that are simply slowing you down to consider "what's possible" and "what's next." You may just be on the road to transformation!

MASTERING PLAN "BE"

✤ Accept that change is inevitable and triggers an emotional reaction.

✤ Plan your change. But manage the transition, too. Otherwise, when you look over your shoulder, no one will be there. They'll be resisting and sabotaging your change. And dealing with that fallout will become your new job.

✤ Acknowledge the emotional part of any change by not only asking others what they *think* about the changes but how they *feel* about them. Be equally aware of your own feelings.

✤ Remember that the first reactions to change begin with grieving the loss of *what* was and the need to let go of that. Allow that in yourself and others.

✤ Use the uncertain time between *what was* and *what will* be to get creative and explore possibilities.

✤ Be patient with yourself and others as you work through the emotional part of the change. The person who knows of the change first is often further ahead with the emotional acceptance and adjustment than those learning of it later.

CHAPTER 2

BE PREPARED FOR TRANSITION FOG

"It is not the clear-sighted who rule the world. Great achievements are accomplished in a blessed, warm fog."
—JOSEPH CONRAD

WITH THREE DIFFERENT early career work experiences under my belt—junior high school teacher fresh out of college, business communications trainer for a small firm, and corporate leader—I then spent fifteen blissful years as an independent consultant. It was the perfect setup. I got to do work I loved with clients I loved. I had the privilege of working out of my home office, and that always afforded me the freedom and flexibility to integrate my work life and home life nicely. It was easy to coordinate schedules with my husband as we each fluidly pursued our careers. I could support my clients through their transitions while still being there for my sons as they navigated their own transitions. It was the best of all worlds.

Until it wasn't.

In 2008, the economy took a nosedive and so did my life, leaving me a divorced mother of two young boys and having to use my change management skills on myself and my own life. Everything as I knew it came undone in that time frame.

A fog rolled in. A fog made up of emotions and uncertainty. I knew everything was about to change. But I couldn't see the path that would take me safely to the other side. I was in a transition fog.

Plan A had been an illusion. It was plan B time. So, I not only ultimately left our house and closest neighborhood friends behind, but I also decided to accept a job offer from one of my clients. The job provided some guaranteed income, benefits, and a place to belong during my life change.

Moving from my consulting role, full of freedom and flexibility, to an employee status was a big adjustment. I mourned my loss of freedom and flexibility. I couldn't be as available to my sons. The short commute to my home office became a lengthy commute over an hour away through sixty—yes, sixty—red lights. The rhythm of my life had surely been disrupted and somehow that commute symbolized the disruption.

I was on the uncertainty road from *what was* to *what would be* and my emotions were right there in the passenger seat as a thick, dense fog rolled in.

WHAT IS TRANSITION FOG?

I call it *transition fog*—when we can't see what's ahead clearly and can't imagine how we're going to navigate a time of change. Transition fog results from the physiological, psychological, and emotional reactions that the change stirs up. It can roll in from a seemingly positive event that you've chosen, like taking a new job, or from an unexpected event, like losing a job. We have no way of knowing just what the road ahead looks like in either case.

The fog is made up of two elements: our *not knowing* and our *emotions*. We grieve what was, feel anxious about our current uncertain circumstances, and fear what's around the bend. The not knowing triggers negative self-talk and emotions—doubt, hopelessness, fear. This can muddy our ability to think clearly and plan. And the not knowing what to do next can paralyze us, or at best, make us feel like our feet are firmly planted in midair.

What's the fog that's rolling in and disorienting *you*? What's your situation? You may be going through a merger or acquisition and wondering about the outcome. You may foresee a company downsizing and wonder if you'll survive the cut. Or, as an entrepreneur, you may be ready to take some risks and expand your business, which has you feeling both excited and unsettled. You may find yourself with a recent promotion and new responsibilities that leave you in new and unknown territory, trying to maintain your positive professional reputation. Perhaps your fog is about a retirement, a shake-up with the board, or a shake-up on the home front. Even a shift in responsibilities can create fog. For example, the need to increase your work travel can make you wonder how in the world you'll balance your personal life with your work life.

Is your fog the thick, intense type of fog resulting from a sudden death or health scare? These can be the get-off-the-road-for-a-while variety resulting from some big, unexpected, or even catastrophic change in your life. This thick fog can bring you to a complete stop, leaving you paralyzed, numb, and stuck.

Or perhaps your fog is more like a low-lying fog that poses a mild disruption on your commute. Perhaps it's a new project assignment or needing to figure out how to work with a new coworker. Or perhaps it's going back to school and wondering how you'll juggle it along with work.

Whether thick or low-lying, fog leaves us disoriented and brings with it emotion that can obscure our view. What feelings are obscuring your view? Grief, anger, frustration, anxiety, worry?

As you sit with your transition fog, you may find yourself wondering, "*Why is this happening?*" "*Now what?*" "*What should I do?*"

"How should I handle this?" "Is this good or bad?" "Where is this leading?" You really want to know. You want answers. But when you're in transition fog, you can't really know where things will end up or how you'll come through it. You crave clarity, but it eludes you.

As a leader this gets compounded. After all, your team and organization expect you to know, well, *everything!* In times of uncertainty, they look to you as their leader. They expect you to have answers to these questions. They want to derive comfort from *your knowing.* They expect you to help them manage their emotions.

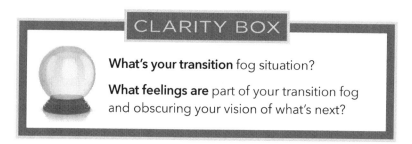

CLARITY BOX

What's your transition fog situation?

What feelings are part of your transition fog and obscuring your vision of what's next?

I recall showing up for an executive coaching session with a CEO of a midsized company. The client was already sitting at the small round table that we typically sat at for our meeting. He was facedown, arms splayed in front of him. He didn't even look up until I sat down. He eventually dragged himself to an upright position, inhaled and exhaled deeply, and began to reflect on the fog he and his organization were facing—budget issues, an industry in flux, and the likelihood of layoffs.

He confessed, "Do you know how many people marvel that I know all that I know? They're *amazed* at my ability to lead us through these ever-changing, complicated times. They credit me with being *so* smart. And yet if they only knew that the only thing I *really* know is how to do my best at figuring it out as I go. I'm often only one step ahead of things."

We decided that it would be important for him to prepare his senior leadership team to help him lead the organization through the complicated time ahead. They ultimately invested a lot of time and energy in creating a strategy and ensuring they were on the same page, speaking in one unified leadership voice, and creating confidence in the organization by their actions. Their fog didn't clear quickly, but they did navigate the organization successfully through it.

I appreciated my client's raw candor. Even CEOs feel vulnerable and uncertain. You may feel the same way at times. Or perhaps you've always assumed that others have some superpower for seeing the future. In my experience, that's just not true.

It's not until you begin to navigate your way through the fog that the uncertainty begins to clear. There's simply no route around it. You need to go through it!

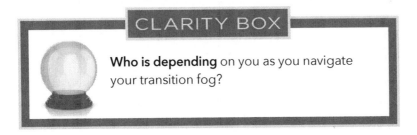

CLARITY BOX

Who is depending on you as you navigate your transition fog?

FOG REDEFINED

If we think of fog as a cloud at ground level, where's the silver lining?

There is one. I experienced it in grad school. I attended a graduate school program with a cohort group of thirty-three of us. We travelled from across the country to spend one long weekend a month together for two years. We were a diverse group of people tossed together for higher education. And we morphed into our own little dysfunctional family system. Given our course of study in organization dynamics, the program was designed to help us learn as much from those dysfunctional experiences as from the textbooks we were reading. So, when things got rough, we used a sort of shorthand. It wasn't uncommon for one us to pronounce, "Ugh, not another FOG!" And we all knew what that meant: another "F@#! %*! Opportunity for Growth." We knew that in the end we'd grow and learn from it, but going through it was not fun.

Yes, Transition FOG is a Freaking Opportunity for Growth.

It may not feel like it when you're travelling through it, but that's the silver lining. This uncertainty and fog provides you with an opportunity to grow. Without it, you'd be stagnant or complacent. You might even be tempted to accept things as "good enough." Your organization is doing "well enough." Your relationship is "good enough." Your health is "okay." Change kicks us out of accepting what is and moves us along a road to what might be better.

I now know that temporarily leaving my consulting practice to take a position with a client organization was a major plan B. And a transition fog really did overtake me. I couldn't imagine how I was going to run my new life under these new circumstances. I couldn't see what was coming or imagine how and where I'd end up. However, it was also a fog in that it was a tremendous opportunity for growth. It led me on a path toward some extremely beneficial experiences that could only be learned from inside an organization as a leader again. It provided me with a chance to live what I thought I knew—and to become a more enlightened consultant who wasn't coaching others based on theory alone, but who had recently "been there." I got to put myself in my clients' shoes—applying what I knew, following my own coaching, and seeing what resulted. It also connected me to an organization and gave me a place to belong during a time when I didn't know where I fit. The people there became dear friends and family and a part of my growth and healing. Looking back, I wouldn't have had it any other way.

It's usually not until you are sitting comfortably in your new reality that'll you be able to look in the rearview mirror to see how this change may have had a positive effect on you and others. But the silver lining is that your fog can lead you to positive outcomes and growth.

Fog can roll in on us as individuals or it can roll in on our organizations. But take heart. I've had some interesting findings with my clients. Years ago, I engaged a group of senior leaders and past clients from some major organizations in an interview process, and a major theme emerged. When asked about the *highlight of their careers*, they discussed a transformational shift that had been born out of a time of craziness and confusion—a professional or organizational *crisis*. It turns out those challenging business situations created opportunities for these leaders and their organizations to become even better. Let me underscore that—their trips through the fog led them to what they reflected on as the *highlight* of their careers. Perhaps that's true for you or your organization right now, despite how it feels.

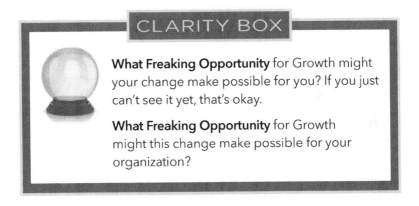

CLARITY BOX

What Freaking Opportunity for Growth might your change make possible for you? If you just can't see it yet, that's okay.

What Freaking Opportunity for Growth might this change make possible for your organization?

NAVIGATING TRANSITION FOG

Okay, so now you know what transition fog is and that it can actually serve you somehow if you're open to that possibility. But in the meantime, how do you navigate the stuff?

We navigate this emotional fog the same way we'd drive in real-life road fog. Think about your instincts.

1. Slow down.

You'd like to get to your destination as soon as possible, but you know that realistically, you need to take it slowly. The trip often feels painfully slow; however, here's an interesting fact. Even though we slow down when driving through fog, we're often moving faster than we realize. Fog actually has an impact on our speed perception. Our brains typically judge speed in contrast to our surroundings, like trees or buildings flashing past in our peripheral vision. But in foggy conditions, contrast is greatly reduced, giving us the perception that we're driving slower than we actually are. So, take heart that when navigating transition fog, we really are making more headway and progress than we realize, even though it may not feel that way.

After all, when we're sick, we can't imagine feeling well. When we begin a new job, we can't imagine ever feeling knowledgeable. When we move, we can't imagine ever feeling at home in the new surroundings. But eventually, we do.

2. Turn your low beams on!

Your high beams are useless. Turning your high beams on only obscures your view and illuminates the fog. It doesn't pay to try to see too far in front of you. You simply can't. Turns out, your low beams are enough. They illuminate the road immediately in front of you. They help you to see a path about 350 feet in front of you. So, you take your journey about 350 feet at a time, focusing your attention on what you *can* see and not worrying about what you can't see. You can safely maneuver small stretches of road at a time and ultimately get to your destination.

When we're experiencing or leading a big change, we have a limited view of how things will go. We may know *what* we want the result to be, but the *how* and *when* we'll get there is less clear. The ultimate outcome is TBD. We just have to trust our GPS, which prompts us turn by turn. We'll take a closer look at this in chapter three.

3. Get off the road!

If the fog is especially thick, there are other options. Have you ever pulled over to the side of the road during fog? Safety experts actually recommend that it's much safer to get completely *off* the road, ideally to a parking lot, and wait for the fog to clear. Your transition may require coming to a temporary halt to let some of your emotional fog clear before beginning to move forward. That could look like simply being patient with yourself or putting some move off until you can gather more information or see how to navigate this uncertain situation.

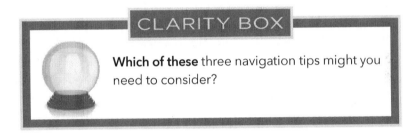

CLARITY BOX

Which of these three navigation tips might you need to consider?

BEWARE OF POTHOLES

Now, what would a good foggy drive metaphor be without some unexpected potholes? Potholes? Yes, I'm calling them that because just like potholes, these phenomena often pop up out of nowhere. They're hard to see in the dark or the fog. And if you don't dodge them, they will most certainly make your trip even trickier.

Here are three common potholes to be on the lookout for.

1. Negative self-talk

When the fog rolls in, our vision of the path forward is obscured. But often our vision of ourselves is obscured, too. Perhaps you've lost a job, lost a client, messed up a business deal, or struggled with a health issue. Fear takes over and that voice in your head forgets who you really are. It turns on you. It "shoulds" all over you. It harps at you that you *should* be adjusting faster, *should* be dealing with it better, *should* know what to do. As your mind swirls, processes, and berates, all you can think is "now what?" It judges that you are worthless, deserved this, aren't good enough, or don't have what it takes to weather this storm. You begin to believe it. And the fog thickens.

Apply your brakes. Find a friend or coworker to shed some light on this pothole before it swallows you up. Keep company with others who can redirect you and remind you of who you are at your core. They will remind you of your accomplishments, value, special qualities, and worth during a time when you can't remember on your own. They will ease your fears.

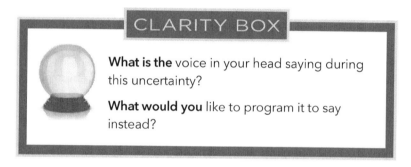

CLARITY BOX

What is the voice in your head saying during this uncertainty?

What would you like to program it to say instead?

2. Comparing yourself to others

When we're struggling, we assume that we're the only ones experiencing this. In our minds, others seem to have it all together. It's natural to compare ourselves to others. I still catch myself doing this and having to reel it in. Nothing good can come from it because the comparisons aren't accurate. At best, we can compare what we actually *know* to be true in our own situation or life with our *perception* of what's true in someone else's life or situation. It's a distorted comparison. We can't ever really know what's going on in someone else's reality. I'm reminded of this time and time again in my role as trusted confessor to clients. I've heard doctors of psychology share surprising facts about their home lives, executives about their inadequacies, and global leaders about serious home issues. I bear secrets that friends have shared with me about situations their own family members aren't aware of. In none of these cases would anyone have ever guessed their struggles.

Again, apply your brakes. The fact is, as humans, we all have struggles. As leaders, we all have struggles. We may not have our respective struggles synced up with others. But none of us lives a trouble-free, fog-free life—despite our titles, incomes, appearances, lifestyles, or public personae. (Pick up a *People* magazine or newspaper if you need proof.)

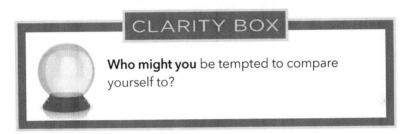

CLARITY BOX

Who might you be tempted to compare yourself to?

3. Impatience

When times are uncertain, we want to move through them *quickly.* So, we lament our slow progress and the long road ahead of us. We can easily fall into the trap of beating ourselves up and discrediting any slow progress we are making. That negative self-talk only brings fear, anxiety, and stress with it. In fact, it makes the journey even slower as we get twisted up in our frustration. We count the miles left before we might be out of the fog. But what about the distance we've already travelled?

Dodge this tendency. Instead, slow down just enough to tick off the progress you are making. Take time at the end of each day to acknowledge any headway you've made. You can do a mental checklist or journal about it. We tend to get more of what we focus on. So, avoid focusing on what's not right, on your frustration, or on your lack of progress. You don't want to slow this trip down even further. The more you pay attention to your headway, the more headway you will make. Perhaps you're working to improve your presentation skills. It's as important to note where you are improving as it is to note where you may still want to improve.

If you can't see it, others do. Just ask them. It will be easy for them to note your headway through the fog. Let them bring it into clear view for you. And then generously do the same for your coworkers, friends, and family members.

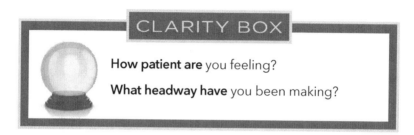

CLARITY BOX

How patient are you feeling?

What headway have you been making?

COMPASSION FOR OTHERS' TRANSITION FOG

Fog doesn't discriminate. It rolls in on leaders. But it also rolls in on your employees. You are entrusted with running a business, but you're also entrusted with the people in the business. They, in turn, are dealing with their own fogs. As a leader, you can't forget that. It may be obvious in situations where they are making a work transition—as in the case of a new employee or corporate attorney trying to negotiate a tricky contract. But fog doesn't know boundaries. It can show up on the work front or the home front. They may be dealing with it privately, and you may never know about it. Even if you do, there may not be anything you can do about it. But simply keep that in the back of your mind as a possibility when unusual reactions, behaviors, and performance show up in otherwise dependable and predictable employees or colleagues.

Here's a sampling of true-life scenarios I've witnessed people struggling with. I'm not sure that their leaders knew what they were dealing with, but these are some serious struggles and fogs. There was the employee who worked with an organization for twenty-two years, was diagnosed with acute lymphoma, and was valiantly battling through it. There was the newly-promoted frontline leader who learned his fifteen-year-old daughter was pregnant. There was the employee whose son committed a crime that landed him in federal prison. There are the employees taking care of aging parents who've had serious falls and health issues. What about the newly-employed woman who left a situation of domestic violence and was moving from a shelter into her first apartment with her three children? May your own experience of change and transition fog bring you to a place of leadership compassion for others as they navigate their own uncertainties.

MASTERING PLAN "BE"

✤ No matter how frustrating it feels, see your FOG for what it is: a Freaking Opportunity for Growth.

✤ Turn on your low beams while navigating this transition fog and focus on what's in view. You can't see where this is taking you yet.

✤ Take your time. It will feel you are moving too slowly, but you're making more headway than you know.

✤ Turn down the volume on the negative voice in your head that may distract you in these complex times.

✤ Avoid comparing your reality with your perception of other's reality. It's an inaccurate comparison. We can never know what others are experiencing.

✤ Dedicate time at the end of each day to acknowledge progress you have made.

✤ Show compassion for others who may be navigating their own fogs.

CHAPTER 3

BE FOCUSED ON THE "NEXT RIGHT THING"

"I long to accomplish a great and noble task; but, it is my chief duty to accomplish small tasks as if they were great and noble."
—HELEN KELLER

I WAS FLANKED BY both of my boys in church one Sunday. That hour-long service was the only predictable hour of most weeks during the time of our crumbling, morphing family life. I loved the familiar flow of the service that always began with announcements by our pastor. That Sunday, he was announcing what they termed a Mission/Vision trip to South Africa. It was a combination of serving, touring, and learning in South Africa. I had always had a strong yearning to go to Africa. I'd always felt an inexplicable connection to this continent and a country that I knew little about really, except that it was called a "land of contrasts"—deep beauty intermingled with great need and pain.

As I sat there soaking up Pastor Steve's invitation, I felt my oldest son leaning toward me. He whispered, "What do you say, Mom? You, me, and South Africa. You know you've always wanted to go."

My eyes met his. I was taken aback. Had my thoughts been so loud he could hear them? Where was this coming from? He and I had never discussed this. Besides, how could I possibly entertain such a crazy idea in the midst of uncertain times, financial and otherwise?

Yet, some part of me loved the idea of twelve special days with my teenage son and the chance to put our life events into perspective. As I tossed and turned with indecision, the signs that we were meant to go came hard at me. And so we signed up, getting the very last two spots left, as a further sign of confirmation. It became plan "be." A chance to just *be* when I wasn't sure what to *do* next.

Months later, we found ourselves bumping along on a bus in South Africa, alternately passing beautiful countryside and shanty town huts huddled under corrugated tin roofs. We were heading toward Nkosi's Haven, a village established for HIV-positive mothers and their children. It wasn't on our original itinerary, but a last minute change made it possible for us to visit. I had wanted to visit this spot so badly that I think I single-handedly willed that change in our itinerary to happen. I was not disappointed. We met with its founder Gail Johnson, an amazing character of a woman. I had "met" Gail and read about her adopted son Nkosi in our pre-reading for the trip: James Wooten's book, *We Are All the Same*.[4] And I had heard a lecture by Wooten at our local university.

Nkosi was a mix of little boy, big brown eyes, and old soul. He was eleven years old and South Africa's longest surviving child born HIV positive. He was slated to speak at the opening ceremony of the 13th International AIDS Conference in Durban in July of 2000. Leading up to his speaking engagement, he was interviewed by ABC news journalist, James Wooten, who immediately fell under the spell of this little man. Wooten says he could never stray far from him after that. Wooten had reported on unthinkable world atrocities and found a way to distance himself emotionally, but he admitted that he couldn't leave the gaze of those big brown eyes for long without returning to visit.

On one of those visits, Wooten was explaining to Nkosi how helpless he felt each time he returned to South Africa, wishing he could make a difference. But the challenges there were complex—political, economic, health-related, and educational. As he lamented his paralysis, Nkosi, much like my son that day in church, leaned in close to this adult.

"Oh, Jim. You're making it *way* too hard," Nkosi stated matter-of-factly. "It's easy."

"Easy?" replied Wooten with curiosity.

"Yes, Jim. It's quite easy. You just do the *next right thing*. That's all." And with that advice, the conversation appeared to be over. Nothing more to say, really.

Sadly, AIDS took Nkosi at age twelve in the year 2001, but not before he had a profound effect on so many others. His adoptive mother Gail opened Nkosi's Haven, offering holistic care and support for destitute HIV/AIDS infected mothers, their children, and the resulting AIDS orphans.

The effect on me? I simply took this wise counsel under advisement. From the time I heard this story, it's never left me. It's been one of the mantras that has seen me through tough, foggy times to this day: "Brenda, just do the next right thing."

DOING THE "NEXT RIGHT THING"

When times are hard and uncertain, when we find ourselves paralyzed, we need to keep it simple. Complicated times call for simple solutions. There's only one question to answer: *What's the next right thing to do now?* It makes the complex seem more manageable. We don't have to look too far forward. We can't expect to see through the fog. We just need to keep moving. As the Chinese Proverb says, "Be not afraid of going slowly, be afraid only of standing still."

Whether you're trying to figure out how to move through something as complicated as a culture change in your organization or whether an evening at home has you feeling stressed and distraught, the approach is the same. Pause. Turn your low beams on. Consider your next move. Then take it. This inches you forward a bit at a time.

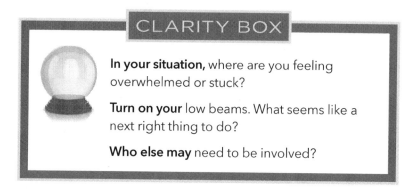

CLARITY BOX

In your situation, where are you feeling overwhelmed or stuck?

Turn on your low beams. What seems like a next right thing to do?

Who else may need to be involved?

Certain next moves may not seem logical.

Next moves may not seem logical to you or others, but that doesn't mean they aren't right. Consider a night where you are stressed over the work you brought home with you. You're already drained from a long, taxing day in the office. When you really think about the next right move, you realize it may be to take a break, relax, and do nothing for an hour. Or maybe you decide to take the night off from work completely and spend it with your family. Doing nothing may not seem logical, but it will have you recharged to take action the next day.

At a time when your organization is going through budget cutbacks, making an investment in a key new hire may not seem logical. But this decision may bring an expertise to the organization that will make some strategic next moves possible.

I've coached leaders who wrestle with whether they should continue investing in their own coaching when their organization is experiencing some belt-tightening. Yet, that's the very time to keep a coach in your corner to help you lead during challenging times.

Trust me, in the early stages of my separation and divorce, booking a trip to South Africa seemed like a next right move in my gut, but it certainly didn't seem very logical. Had I looked at the facts and dollars and "sense" of that decision, I never would have gone. But I listened to that voice in me and that otherworldly voice expressed through my son in church that Sunday. I did what felt right at that time—getting away, getting perspective, and getting reminded that there was a big wide world out there. I experienced the joy of the South African people whose issues seemed more insurmountable than mine. Yet, they radiated joy and carried hope in their hearts. It brought my situation into perspective. It inspired me to keep navigating my transition fog. I could never have imagined the powerful impact that trip would have on me when I signed up. I just knew it was the *next right thing* to do.

When we returned from South Africa, real life was ready and waiting for me. Or should I say the dismantling of one life and the necessary creation of a new one awaited me. It was more *surreal* than *real*. And I had absolutely no idea how I'd manage. But I did. We all do.

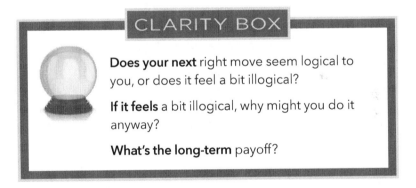

CLARITY BOX

Does your next right move seem logical to you, or does it feel a bit illogical?

If it feels a bit illogical, why might you do it anyway?

What's the long-term payoff?

When others ask how I navigated from the life I had to the one I now have—through the dismantling, uncertainty, and recreating—I can honestly admit that I'm not smarter, more insightful, or a better strategist than most. I've simply done one next right thing after the other over the years. I couldn't always see too far into the future. But I could, in my overwhelm, step back and assess the next right thing. And that made the complex seem more manageable.

Focusing on the next right thing(s), can also keep you from obsessing, stressing, and worrying over the future.

Worrying into the future and obsessing over it can stop you in your tracks. It's not uncommon to get paralyzed with fear. That will only increase your transition fog. Theodore Roosevelt said it best: "I dream of men who take the next step instead of worrying about the next thousand steps." That's the beauty of the next right thing approach. It keeps you from worrying so much about the next thousand steps. It puts you squarely in the power of the present.

That's what one of my past clients, Steve, did. Steve was a client I had worked with before. He called to tell me he had accepted a new position in a pharma organization. But when he got there, he realized he was in over his head. His group was just that: a group. They had never developed into a team. They were distraught having had four leaders over four years and disheartened by not having demonstrated a profit in seven years. Steve took over the group with the motivation to rise to the challenge, but had no idea how he was going to make that happen.

Steve wasn't sure what to do with this group, but he didn't angst over it for long. He could have become overwhelmed with the task ahead of him—creating a cohesive team and turning a profit. Instead, he thought about a strategic next right thing. He needed to reach out for support.

Steve was a finance guy by training and a conscientious, committed leader. I had worked with him in other organizations, so I was happy to hear his voice on the other end of the phone one day. I'll never forget what he said: "I know what I know, Brenda, and I know what I don't know. I'm good on the business end of this challenge, but I don't know where to begin with the people part of it. So, I could struggle with it or just do the one thing I know to do right now: call you to partner with me to turn this place around."

We brought the group together and began to work, one step at a time toward a "better" future for them. Ultimately, they created a strong vision for themselves, defined key values to support getting there, and made clear action plans. Over that year, they developed into a high-performing, cohesive leadership team that proudly reported a profit for the first time in seven years. The profit was not where they put all their focus initially, but it was an understandable byproduct of the steps they did take one-by-one under Steve's leadership. He still reminisces about it as a true highlight of his career.

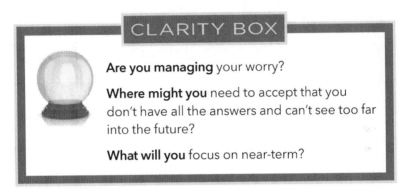

CLARITY BOX

Are you managing your worry?

Where might you need to accept that you don't have all the answers and can't see too far into the future?

What will you focus on near-term?

Steve's story reminds us that just one step, one decision, can keep us from getting stuck. It can create movement. It keeps us from worrying into the future and getting paralyzed. When contracting with clients, I often ask if they are comfortable "building the bridge as we walk on it." Complex situations often require that. You may want to be a bit suspect of the consultant or new leader who comes in suggesting they know just how it's going to go and exactly what needs to be done. Most things related to people aren't that straightforward and predictable.

Focusing on the next right thing continues to pay off, even when the fog begins to lift and you can see farther down the road. Next right things ensure progress.

As you move through your transition, you'll begin to get a clearer picture of what's possible. You'll be able to see the future state you want. You'll set longer-term goals. Clarity is great. Goals are, too. But beware of that sense of accomplishment that can set in after establishing your goals. If those goals are for a one to three year period of time, we can be lulled into a false sense of security that we have plenty of time to reach them.

How often have you set weight loss goals? On New Year's Eve we set a goal to lose fifteen pounds this year. And it seems we have a lot of time before we have to really set our new habits in place. So, the diet and exercise program keeps getting kicked into the future. After all, there are so many tomorrows between now and then. (Tomorrow being the preferred day of the week to start a diet or exercise program.) We actually end up in a state of inactivity because the urgency isn't there. We feel a luxury of time, so we take our focus off of the next steps to get us there. That's the benefit of setting quarterly, monthly, weekly next moves to ensure that you or your team meet that long-range goal. A series of next right things is the only path to your future destination.

I've seen entrepreneurs fall into the trap time and again. I've worked with more than one founder of an organization who has set their sights on retiring in five years. They tell me with great authority about their retirement—the golf, the travel, the relaxation. But they never retire. Years later, they're still at the helm. They set the goal, but they forget to do the next right things to feel comfortable stepping down. (A few of you may be reading this and gulping. And you're more likely reading it on an airplane than a beach.)

So, as your transition fog clears enough for you to see your destination, be sure to set a plan and then use your low beams to carry you through weekly, daily, and hourly next moves to get you there. Thinking short-term actually increases our chances of long-term success. Each day I note three to five actions I commit to taking that day. Sometimes they don't seem very big or meaningful. But it's deceiving. They keep me focused and really add up to progress by the week's end.

A fellow consultant, Keisha, was lamenting to me one December about her fears for the coming year. She had had no client work in view. Her bank account was dwindling, and she felt paralyzed with fear as she tried to find her way through this fog. Extreme anxiety took hold. But when the new year came, she set a financial goal for herself, along with some other key goals related to creative projects and new ventures. She felt a little foolish putting lofty goals down when she couldn't even see where her next check would come from. I visited with Keisha in her office in mid-January. I noted the big mind map she had posted on a flipchart on her wall. When I asked her how things were going, she shared that she had booked 30 percent of the revenue she had set as an annual goal and was making significant progress with each of her numerous projects. I was stunned. How had this woman made that kind of transition so quickly? She began to share that while she couldn't see how she was going to meet those goals, she got busy with manageable next moves like making phone calls to former clients, setting up lunch meetings, and determining next moves in all of her project areas. And she had made some extremely impressive headway. It was hard to reconcile this as the same person I had seen lost in her new year's Transition Fog!

Keisha is proof that some very small immediate actions can lead to major headway. In fact, it's the only thing that's going to get you to that lofty goal you've set or vision you hold, especially when navigating fog. Granted, looking into the future can be preferable to looking at the mess in front of us. The simple near-term actions and steps seem less glamorous. Even worse, they require us to be accountable to action. Yet, dreaming and strategizing about the future is just that—planning. Without action, those plans are nothing but magical thinking. Next right moves serve future goals.

We never feel like we're doing enough, or moving fast enough, or seeing clearly enough. But I see the relief come over the faces of clients, friends, and colleagues when I gently remind them that if they do one next right thing after the other, they will eventually come to the other side of their complexity. I hope you'll find relief in that reminder, too.

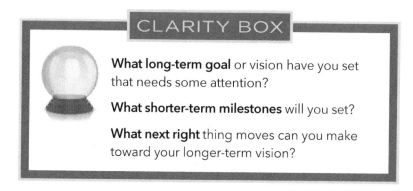

CLARITY BOX

What long-term goal or vision have you set that needs some attention?

What shorter-term milestones will you set?

What next right thing moves can you make toward your longer-term vision?

RECALCULATING

Does this still feel uncomfortable? Does your worry about doing the *wrong* next thing stop you cold? It's easy to get paralyzed during complex times, but I often remind myself, clients, family, and friends that most decisions are reversible. You aren't stuck with them for life. You simply need to do the next right thing *for now*—that thing that will get you moving and out of inertia. Naturally, don't suspend your good judgment. I'm not suggesting careless, reckless actions, but clear, next actions. When we overly focus on the too-distant future, we become overwhelmed with fear. We often think we should wait until we can see the whole plan before acting. But that's like trying to see your destination before you even get in the car. Once we begin moving, our GPS kicks in and shows us options for getting where we want to go. A path forward unfolds.

The *next* right thing may be the polar opposite of an earlier choice you made. Again, it's like that GPS system when you make a wrong turn and hear it groan, "recalculating." We get to recalculate, too. Perhaps you toured fifteen colleges, enrolled your son in one, and then watched him transfer after his freshman year to a college he had never even toured in his search. (Can you tell this isn't all that hypothetical?) That's a recalculation of an earlier decision. Perhaps your work team tried a new way of doing things to streamline a process, but it didn't get the results hoped for. So, you went back to the old way. Or perhaps you bought something online, didn't like it, and returned it. These are reminders that we don't have to be perfect in the steps we take. Perfection is another roadblock to progress. We just do our best at the time and remember we can opt for a necessary do-over in many cases.

One choice at a time, somehow it all works out. We don't have crystal balls. So, we step out in faith. We do the next right thing. And we recalculate if we need to.

During times of change, your team is taking their cues from you. Are you a role model for recalculating? Are you willing to acknowledge fog? Are you willing to say, "I don't know"? A leader who admits this gains respect over the leader who makes up an answer that nobody buys anyway. Do you openly admit to your mistakes? Are you willing to be imperfect?

During change, no matter how well you plan, it's not going to go as planned. Even when you make moves with the best of intentions, they may not work. So, know that up front. There will be bumps in the road. In the fog, your team members may feel paralyzed with worry about making a wrong turn, too. Seeing your willingness to make mistakes, be imperfect, and recalculate will free them to move.

How high is the bar you've set for yourself and others? How easy is it to accept imperfection from your team? What does the conversation sound like with a team member who makes a mistake? Do you talk about others' mistakes or incompetence behind their backs to others? When you do this, others wonder what you say when they aren't in the room. So, it's important to reframe imperfections as opportunities for learning. It's important to maintain the self-esteem of the person who may have made a move that didn't work out. If you overreact to mistakes and treat them as failures, you are bound to paralyze your staff from acting. You will all be stuck in the status quo. All the creativity and possibility that marks the opportunity of the uncertainty state will vanquish. Everyone will have driven off the road to wait for the fog to clear, and that may take a long while. You may be the only one willing to take any action whatsoever.

During transition, you may be inclined to hold the reigns tight and keep control over as much as you can. Avoid that pitfall, and embrace the idea that imperfection will be a necessary evil on the road to *what will be*. Rather than control, let go and recalculate as necessary.

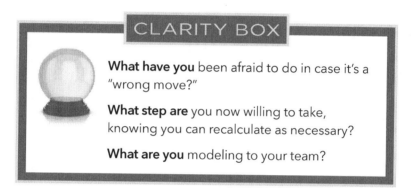

CLARITY BOX

What have you been afraid to do in case it's a "wrong move?"

What step are you now willing to take, knowing you can recalculate as necessary?

What are you modeling to your team?

I worked with a telecommunications center whose new leadership wanted to improve the focus and readiness of their emergency call takers. So, they decided that these phone operators could no longer do puzzles, knit, listen to music, or do most anything in between calls. Leadership wanted to control the environment, make it more "professional," and eliminate all distractions. But it backfired. The call takers grew bored. So, between calls they entertained themselves at the expense of their coworkers. Workplace harassment and unwelcome behavior skyrocketed. After an analysis of the workplace culture, leadership realized that the new policy had created a problem where there hadn't been one before. Leadership needed to recalculate and reinstate the old, more flexible policy. The team respected their leaders' willingness to admit they had misjudged the situation and were willing to do a U-turn. That very department went on to flourish and win statewide recognition for their accomplishments and performance.

Be willing to recalculate because the path forward isn't straight—it's swirly and interesting and full of curves we can't see around.

MASTERING PLAN "BE"

❖ Just do the *next right thing* when the path forward is unclear.

❖ Remember that some next moves don't seem logical.

❖ Stay focused on the present. Worrying about seeing a clear path to the future may become an obstacle to your progress.

❖ Continue to focus on next right thing moves even after the fog begins to clear. Only a series of next right things will get you to your long-term goals.

❖ Embrace wrong moves and imperfection as opportunities to learn and necessary travel companions on the road to *what will be*.

❖ Remember that most decisions are reversible.

❖ Model and accept the need to recalculate when necessary... and keep moving.

CHAPTER 4

BE MINDFUL OF TOPS, MIDDLES, AND BOTTOMS

"Sometimes life in the organization feels like a game of pinball, and we're the little metal ball."
—BARRY OSHRY

MY FIRST CORPORATE position was as an assistant manager of a training and development department. I came on board and worked side by side with my team members, all of whom knew more about the organization, industry, and inner workings of our department than I did. I had a lot to learn, but my teammates were willing and patient teachers, and we worked together with ease. Five months after I joined the team, our manager unexpectedly left the organization. I was asked to take her place and gulped at the idea. I was so new and had so much to learn. I was barely through one transition, and here I was experiencing another one already. But I didn't have too much of a choice. So, I moved into her office.

One day, Connie, whom I had worked closely with for five months as she helped me learn the ropes, came to my office and sat perched on the edge of the chair facing my desk. Her brow was furrowed and her eyes were focused on her lap. Connie and I had had an easy rapport from the start, so I was curious about her demeanor that day. She stumbled over her words, wringing her hands all the while. I prepared myself for some bad news. None came. But she continued to struggle through our conversation. I finally came right out and asked her if everything was okay.

She replied, "It's just that I get so nervous when I have to come in here and talk to you."

Nothing about that answer made sense to me. "Why would you get nervous?" I questioned, wondering what I was missing.

"Well, because you're the *boss* now."

"Connie, I'm just *me*," I replied.

"I know, but it's just different now."

This was my first lesson in the dynamics of an organizational system.

SEEING THE INVISIBLE

As a leader navigating a change and trying to do the next right thing, you will be operating within the context of some invisible system dynamics that you may never have thought about but are important to understand. The turbulence associated with change will only accentuate them. To make conscious moves that make sense, it's important to remember that all of your next moves are taking place within a broader context.

Connie reminded me of that. Nothing had changed about *me* necessarily; it wasn't personal. But what had changed was the dynamic of our relationship where she now saw me as "the boss." I had moved into a different space relative to her space.

What happened? According to Barry Oshry, researcher, author, and pioneer in the field of power and leadership, some invisible forces were playing out. He calls them "system dynamics."* That's a fancy term for a group of interdependent people who coexist with each

---

* The conceptual framework underlying this chapter is based on the work of Barry Oshry. See especially *Seeing Systems: Unlocking the Mysteries of Organizational Life*, Berrett-Koehler, San Francisco, 2007.

other and the "stuff" that plays out among them. Examples of systems include organizations, teams, schools, families, and communities.

Within them are spaces Oshry calls tops, middles, bottoms, and customers. And while we could overlay these positions on an org chart where they correlate with hierarchy, we all move in and out of these spaces all day every day depending on whom we're interacting with.

Let's take a closer look at the two spaces that leaders often occupy: the top leadership space and the middle leadership space. *How* we occupy these spaces can make a significant difference for leading during uncertainty and mitigating the vulnerability that others experience at the hands of change.

THE TOP SPACE

Are you the one everyone turns to for answers? Do you feel the weight of the world on your shoulders. Do you suffer some restless nights? If so, you're most likely occupying the top space. *The top space is a space full of complexity and responsibility.* During uncertain times, that complexity and responsibility gets amplified.

If you're a parent, you understand top space. I'll never forget that moment when we were leaving the hospital with our newborn son, putting him in his car seat, and then driving him through the traffic and away from the medical experts. There was nothing like the realization that this little guy's life and well-being was squarely our responsibility to bring the concept of top space into full view.

As a leader, employees depend on you for their well-being, too. They may see you as the one with all the answers. The thing is, there's just too much to do and so little time. And because tops are looking out for the big picture—scanning the external environment, assessing the competition, responding to the board or Wall Street— they can't help but get removed and disconnected from realities deeper in the organization. This only adds to transition fog.

During times of change and uncertainty, there are some top space pitfalls to avoid and possibilities to consider.

Pitfall #1: Sucking it up

You may react to the responsibility you feel during change by taking it all on yourself—by sucking it up. As a result, you'll feel even more burdened. This can begin a vicious cycle that doesn't benefit you or anyone else. The fact is, you can't know all the answers, figure it all out alone, and then do it all.

Try this:

Share the responsibility. Involve others. Sucking it up keeps others from learning some important skills. If you're always tying your son's shoes, he'll never learn to do it himself. If you're always thinking for your team, they'll never develop critical thinking skills. When we inadvertently suck the responsibility up and always take care of things, our family members and coworkers are happy to let us (and then blame us if things don't go well). So, share the responsibility.

Here's how it's done:

I was once engaged as a consultant by a Physical Therapy department undergoing a needed reorganization. The leader, Ted, could have taken the responsibility upon himself to compose a new org chart and structure, but he realized his team was in a better position than he was to know what was best for the department and how it functioned. So, rather than race through the uncertainty stage to the *what will be* stage, together, we created an approach that would engage the members of the department in creating their own structure. Ted selected members of the department who would be the working group. Their job would be to create a proposed new structure. He provided them with clear directions and set them loose. I met with them for a few sessions. Each session ended with a timeslot where other leaders from the department, as well as leaders from outside the department who might be affected by the new structure, joined us. We'd brief them on the group's progress and thinking. The guest leaders would then share what they liked about what they heard, as well as what we called "please considers," which were possible suggestions. Over time, I eased out of the workgroup, and they continued the work quite capably. A new structure surfaced. The new structure was not the only thing to celebrate. How it came about was something to celebrate, too. The executive that this group reported to was so pleased that he wanted to share the approach with the executive team. It was an example of sharing responsibility with a team and empowering them, rather than having a top leader impose a new structure on them. The result? A structure that everyone bought into and felt proud about. It took longer, but it was well worth it.

Pitfall #2: Guarding turf

Leave it on the athletic field. It may be ideal for the performance of competing athletes, but it doesn't serve teams of tops. Because there's so much to deal with in organizations, dividing and conquering makes complete sense. Someone can head up HR, Finance, Marketing, etc. But in time, we can fall into the trap of thinking that we "own" our area, that we are rulers of our fiefdoms, and that we're not beholden to ideas or input from our colleagues. We forget we are on the same team. During unsettled times, we especially need our top leaders to be on the same page. And we can really benefit from sharing input and ideas across our functional areas.

I learned this lesson on the home front. We once got locked out of our home. I remember my husband and I racing around the house, hopeful we'd find an unlocked door or window. This went on for a long time with no success. Exasperated, we got back in the car where our four-year-old son was hanging out, watching our performance. At a loss, we began to talk about a way to "break in." A little voice emerged from the back seat: "Guys, can't we just get the key from the cleaning lady?" (Who happened to live close by.) We thought figuring out how to get in the house was part of parental turf. But it turns out that insights can come from others outside our "territory" if we are open to it.

Try this:

Consider yourself a guardian of your area of expertise, not the ruler. Be open to others' input and ideas. Contribute across boundaries to your colleagues' work as well. Remember that you each work for the same system, not multiple systems. Seeing you working as one team will bring great comfort to the rest of the organization.

Here's how it's done:

One of the best examples I have of being conscious about how to work in top space for the good of a whole system occurred in a large school district in suburban Philadelphia that I got to work closely with behind the scenes during a major change. The district was growing at a rapid pace, and building space was over capacity. It became clear that they had to move from a one-high-school to a two-high-school system. That was going to be a complex change and impact thousands of students and families. On top of that, faculty were going to have their worlds turned upside down. It was also going to take one tight-knit community and potentially split it in two. Frankly, it had the potential to be a big mess.

The district superintendent named the individuals who would be the principals of those two schools and then formed a steering committee comprised of top leadership in the district. The group worked with several key goals in mind that overrode any temptation to protect or create turf. They were clear that they would not split the community by creating two high schools that could become unhealthy rivals. They were also emphatic that they would create two demographically balanced schools. They worked across boundaries and areas of expertise to create one impressive school system.

The principals led the charge, talking and acting as one unified team and sending a clear message about the importance of partnership in the culture. Leadership engaged the faculty and other stakeholders in the planning. They were careful in the naming of the schools, using the same name and simply adding East and West to the ends of the names. They carefully constructed overlap among the schools, students, and community: bands that performed together, a ninth grade center that comingled the students before they headed to the high schools, and so much more. They adopted the tagline "16 great schools, one caring community." I was honored to be part of this amazing example of what's possible if we work across turf and are mindful of system dynamics. The district continues to grow and morph in impressive ways. In 2017, it was the only multi-high school district in Pennsylvania to have all of its high schools appear on the Washington Post's elite list of America's Most Challenging programs.[5] And they now have three high schools ranked #1, #19, and #29 of the 952 public high schools in Pennsylvania. That's a big accomplishment.

Eliminating turf can happen through small measures, too. I've seen a leadership team that operated quite comfortably in their own world get shaken up (in a good way) by a new member who found her new team's turf-like ways odd. Her new team members often worked behind closed doors, knew relatively little about one another's families, and didn't do much to celebrate special events like birthdays. This energetic and personable young leader of strategy began to shift the team in small ways. She planted a basket of snacks in her office to encourage others to come see her more often. She made sure birthday cards were purchased and signed by the team for each birthday. She and her husband had a love for cooking and often entertained team members at their home, cooking favorite dishes from their culture. She played an important role in bringing people together and helping to shift the team dynamics. All you have to do is sign into her *Facebook* page to see the evidence of these team gatherings and events. These small inroads can make a big difference in team members getting more comfortable bringing the walls down and working more readily across functional areas.

Pitfall #3: Being disconnected and out-of-touch

Top leaders are often appropriately focused on issues external to the organization. And depending on the size and culture of the organization, it can be difficult for others to get access to tops. Much of the information that comes to tops is funneled up and highly filtered. All of this contributes to the likelihood of being disconnected from some of the realities in the organization. Yet, some of those realities are important to factor in as you lead others through change.

Try this:

Get connected. During times of change, top leaders need to be more visible. Employees are already dealing with transition fog. Leadership presence can help to mitigate the fear of what they can't see or know. Seeing you and engaging with you helps smooth over some of the vulnerability they are experiencing.

Here's how it's done:

Connecting with others can happen on a big scale, like arranging town hall sessions to keep others updated, answer questions, and solicit reactions during times of change and transition. It can also help to simply come out of your office more often. Use your commute between meetings for hallway engagement with others. Avoid the temptation to fixate on your phone while in transit. Connect and chat with others. Or make it a point to eat in the cafeteria, avoiding your temptation to sit with your peers. Instead, make yourself open and accessible to others. I used to spend an hour working at a table in the cafeteria each day. It's amazing how much I learned and how much I got done. All the face time with others eliminated emails and phone calls I would have had to make.

Another way of staying connected was instituted by one of my client groups. They called it leadership rounding. Leaders were required to have monthly one-on-one conversations with their direct reports. They used a list of topics and questions to guide the conversation. The questions ranged from "Who would you like to acknowledge for their good work this month?" to "Do you have the resources you need to do your work right now?" Direct reports appreciated the one-on-one attention, and it kept leaders from getting too out-of-touch with reality.

Pitfall #4: Underutilizing middle managers

When tops fall prey to pitfall #1, sucking responsibility up, middles become little more than disempowered order-takers. But even if that's not the case, middles often feel less informed about what's happening in times of change than they'd like to be, limiting their ability to make a positive difference. From the unique role in the middle of the organization where they interact with tops, bottoms, and even customers, middle managers are key information cogs—both up and down the organization. Others in the organization look to them for information. They are a go-to group for many and can ease concerns during times of uncertainty, provided they have adequate information to share. It's imperative.

Try this:

Keep your middles informed. They need to have direction and information to help lead during times of transition. Use them as conduits of information that others need to know. And invite them to be reality-checkers of your ideas and plans. Encourage their coming together—"integration" with other middles—to work smarter and provide tops with important intelligence.

How it's done:

I was approached by an executive who worked for a national non-profit organization and oversaw their activities in a southern US state. Their goal was to refresh a three-year strategic plan that had been put in place the prior year. The original plan was devised by this executive with some input from others, but had been leader-created for the most part. She had been new and needed to pull that plan together quickly. That year, she wanted to be more inclusive than ever. So, she and her senior leader counterpart used specific criteria to carefully select individuals who played very different roles in the organization. These individuals came together, travelling from all areas of the state. They met in person numerous times over three months in what we call a Leadership Action Lab to co-create the new strategy plan. Between sessions, they did other work and engaged other stakeholders across the organization for input. They shared their unique perspectives, had healthy debate, created a shared vision, and grew quite invested in the organization's future. Never had this type of coordination taken place before in that organization. The results were exciting and the top leaders were able to share responsibility with those in the middle of the organization, all the while building a strong commitment to the vision. The strategic plan presented to the board carried even more credibility as a result of their thoughtful engagement of their middle managers.

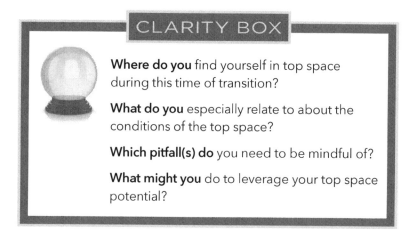

CLARITY BOX

Where do you find yourself in top space during this time of transition?

What do you especially relate to about the conditions of the top space?

Which pitfall(s) do you need to be mindful of?

What might you do to leverage your top space potential?

Being aware of the dynamics we can fall prey to when in top space is important. Understanding middle space dynamics is equally important. Each space comes with its own unique dilemmas, pitfalls, and contributions during times of uncertainty.

THE MIDDLE SPACE

How do you know when you're in middle space? If you are running between groups of tops, bottoms, and customers and trying to make everyone happy (and failing), you're likely in middle space. As Oshry writes in *Seeing Systems*, "Middles are pulled between the often conflicting needs, requests, demands, and priorities of those above them and those below them."[6] *The middle space is a space full of tearing.* You spend time interacting with people in other spaces who are all too happy to tell you what they need and want—which just so happens to be in direct opposition to what others need and want. What *you* think seems to get lost in all the pleasing you're trying to do. And well, frankly, you may not always feel like you are doing a very good job. It can feel pretty lonely. During uncertain times, that gets amplified as others come to you for answers—answers that you may not have. You only know what you're being told and you spend more time interacting with your boss and your direct reports in your silo than anyone else, so your view of the bigger picture is limited. All of this is typical of the dynamics of the middle space.

You probably know the middle space quite well. Hierarchically speaking, you may sit in the middle of the organization between folks you report to and others whom report to you. Even CEOs are middle to the board and the rest of the organization. You may find yourself stuck in the middle between two colleagues who don't get along. You may find yourself in the middle between a customer and a policy your company has. You may often feel torn and in the middle as you try to split your time between the demands of work and the demands of family. As the holidays roll around you try to create a plan to keep both your parents and your in-laws happy. It's a clear indication that you are squarely in middle space.

If you're a middle manager, there are four powerful ways that you can serve the organization during uncertain times. Doing these will close the "us/them" gap, make important information available for good decision-making, and ease the concerns of others.

1. Integrate with other middles.

In other words, break down the silos. When middles come together it's powerful. No boss in the room, just middle peers. It's a chance to get real, compare notes across the middle of the organization, compare what you see happening in your respective areas and put pieces of the bigger puzzle together. That sharing of perspectives, problems, and concerns will bring a new intelligence to the organization. You'll be able to do some great problem solving and generate creative solutions. You'll find support from this group and be in a better position as integrated middles to speak and act consistently—and in one voice—to tops and bottoms. This unity will be evident to others and will create some stability during a time when things feel unsettled. Warning: it will NOT be easy to get middles to meet. Middles are torn in many different directions. It will require a sacred commitment by all members. But a group of well-integrated middles can have far more impact than you can working in isolation and trying to be heard or to make a difference.

2. Be the best communication pipeline possible.

Middles forget the critical role they play in keeping communication flowing during uncertain times. As a middle, you are in a position to both share information with direct reports and learn from them. What you learn is the information to take to your integration meetings with your peers. What you take from your peer sessions should be shared with your direct reports. What you learn from tops can be shared by you, too. Middles are invaluable collectors and disseminators of information. During uncertain times, this is a pivotal role.

3. Be a reality-checker to tops.

Tops are often removed from organization realities, more as a function of their role than due to any ineptitude. What they see as a good move may be not be viewed that way by others deeper in the organization or by your customer base. From where you sit as a middle, you may see the reality of how this move may impact or be perceived by others in the organization. Find an appropriate way to bring this reality-check to the tops. It's in service to them and the rest of the organization. Tops might be influenced by what you share and rethink some move, or they may choose to act as planned. No matter. Be a leader who is willing to shed some light on a situation.

4. Take initiative.

When times are uncertain, you may be tempted to wait for clear direction and permission to take certain steps. But you may need to forge your own direction at times. Be willing to make things happen. That may mean you find yourself asking forgiveness on occasion, but it's better than waiting for permission and becoming a bottleneck to progress.

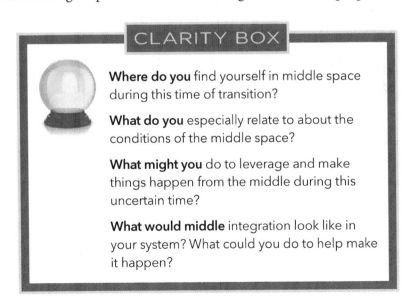

CLARITY BOX

Where do you find yourself in middle space during this time of transition?

What do you especially relate to about the conditions of the middle space?

What might you do to leverage and make things happen from the middle during this uncertain time?

What would middle integration look like in your system? What could you do to help make it happen?

I saw these four middle tips in action during the building and opening of a new hospital. It was a career highlight to have been engaged with this project over a three-year period of time, from inception to opening. Despite excellent planning and preparation, once the doors opened to patients, there was still a lot of uncertainty in the air. To manage through the transition, directors (middle managers) met on a monthly basis. There were no tops in the meetings. The agenda was pretty loose. The meetings were meant to bring these leaders who were very busy and focused on their own departments together. They shared how things were going in their respective departments, noted the themes that were emerging across the organization, supported one another, flagged issues that needed to be raised to top leadership, problem-solved and shared best practices. Some meetings were big celebrations about progress and successes; other meetings were more like good group therapy sessions, complete with frustration, stress, and tears.

But one thing stood out to me about the meetings. Usually, within ten minutes of the meeting invitation going out, the "will attend" replies flew back. This was one meeting no middle wanted to miss. It offered too much value. It was a place where the walls came down, everyone got out of their siloes, and they benefitted from seeing the larger system they were a part of more clearly. Each middle leader felt more informed and less alone for having made the commitment to attend these meetings. Tops benefited from the information, observations, and suggestions they got from this integrated group. Bottoms had the benefit of middle leaders operating in consistent ways and as one team, creating reassurance for them in these early days of operating. Most importantly, the patients and their families reaped the rewards of a safe and more satisfying patient experience that resulted from middle integration.

WHAT TOPS AND MIDDLES NEED TO KNOW ABOUT BOTTOMS

The bottom space is full of vulnerability. Many decisions get made by higher-ups. These decisions affect the bottoms, but the bottoms have no voice in those decisions. As Oshry says, "They often feel unseen and uncared for." They feel "isolated, don't have the big picture."[7] The vulnerability bottoms feel during times of change and uncertainty often shows up in the form of resistance. Given that bottoms are the critical frontline people in the organization and are critical to its success, it's important that tops and middles apply the strategies in this chapter to keep bottoms informed, empowered, and engaged.

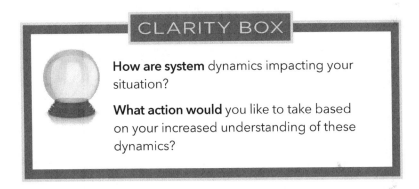

CLARITY BOX

How are system dynamics impacting your situation?

What action would you like to take based on your increased understanding of these dynamics?

System dynamics are alive in every organization, whether you work in a global enterprise, are an entrepreneur, lead a school system, or lead community efforts and committees. Understanding these dynamics can make the difference between feeling like you work on a soap opera or for an extremely strategic and enlightened organization. Being your most strategic self from the top or middle space in an organization is what every day calls for, but times of change especially call for this. You can't fix what you can't see. But once you see systems dynamics at work, you hold the key to new possibilities— and a greater understanding of how *to be* during times of change.

MASTERING PLAN "BE"

❖ Take a good look at the dynamics of your system. Appreciate the unique challenges and contributions top and middle leaders can make during times of change.

❖ Be a top leader who:

- ✓ Shares responsibility, develops, and empowers others during times of change.
- ✓ Puts the good of the whole system before your own turf needs.
- ✓ Keeps middles informed.
- ✓ Gets out of your office and finds opportunity to connect with others during this time of uncertainty.

❖ Be a middle who:

- ✓ Works across siloes and integrates with peers to work smarter and find support.
- ✓ Provides reality checks to tops, appropriately and willingly.
- ✓ Shows initiative and doesn't wait for permission to do so.
- ✓ Keeps information flowing up, down, and across the organization.

❖ Be mindful of the vulnerability that bottoms feel.

CHAPTER 5

BE THINKING ABOUT
WHAT YOU'RE THINKING

*"When you change the way you look at
things, the things you look at change."*
—WAYNE DYER

I ACTUALLY LOVE BUSINESS traveling. There's just something about that literal transition of moving from where I've been to where I'm going. I love being suspended above the world, separate from whatever reality I've just left and the one I'm moving toward on the other end. I love being off-line from Earth and drinking in the sky art. I love that feeling of being still, even though we are racing through space. I do good thinking up there. And interesting things always happen.

Years ago, I shuffled onto a plane taking me from Boston to Philadelphia. I drew closer to my seat in the middle of the plane, noting the weary business travelers intermingled with high school students fresh from summer camp in New England. The business travelers made no noise. The students didn't stop.

I found my less-than-glamorous middle seat in a row of three. My work colleague followed behind me and claimed the aisle seat. On my right was an empty seat. I wasn't expecting it to remain empty. So, I did what we all do in that situation, whether we're aware of it or not. I took stock of the passengers coming down the aisle, giving them a mental thumbs-up or thumbs-down about becoming my seatmate. The person who paused at our aisle was a tall guy with unkempt, curly, black hair, a leather jacket, ripped jeans, heavy boots, and tattoos. After a quick scan, that's what stood out to me—his appearance. In all honesty, I gave him a mental thumbs-down.

There were so many other things I could have noticed about him—the magazine he was carrying, his smile, perhaps some fear in his eyes, but no. My cursory assessment focused on the tattoos and boots and conjured up images of such characters on the evening news making trouble. I concluded I'd have *nothing* in common with this guy.

My "expert" assessment took nanoseconds. My behavior followed suit. I made no eye contact or conversation and took a deep dive into my book.

But here's the thing. At times, circumstances become our teachers. In this case, our plane hit an air pocket and did a quick descent. I'm sure it lasted seconds, but it felt like minutes. Passenger screams filled the cabin. I clutched my book and turned to my work colleague who whimpered, "Please tell me this isn't how it ends." For a moment, I felt like I was part of a bad movie.

When the plane righted itself, and things settled down again, I heard a soft voice on my right. It said, "Excuse me, ma'am, may I ask you a question?"

I glanced at my thumbs-down seatmate and nodded yes.

"Is that not normal?" the tattooed man inquired.

I turned to him and admitted that I travelled a lot and had never had that experience before.

He replied, "Oh, I wouldn't know. This is my *first* flight. I've always been afraid of flying. But, ya see, my parents are getting up in years, and they've always *longed to see the foliage in New England*." I swear those were his exact words! He continued, "So, I had no choice but to drive them safely to New England to explore. But the thing is, my baby turns three tomorrow, and Daddy doesn't miss his baby's birthday for anything," he said in a sing-songy way. "So, I had no choice but to hop on a plane."

Now, wait. What just happened?

Brenda to radio control. I could use some help here.

Well, to understand, we'll need to look for answers in that little black box we'll call my brain. In it, we'll find a ladder. It's a ladder you all have in your black box brains, too. And we climb it all day long.

This ladder is called the Ladder of Inference.[8]

THE LADDER OF INFERENCE
AND MAKING UP STORIES

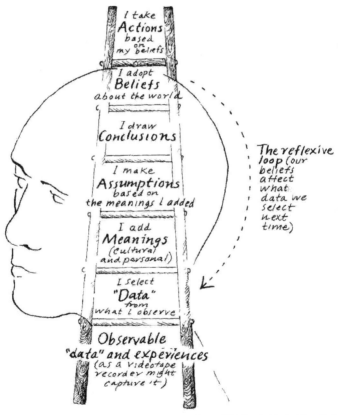

Used by permission of Rick Ross, PhD, and Charlotte Roberts, PhD. Credit: The Ladder of Inference was first put forward by organizational psychologist Chris Argyris and used by Peter Senge in The Fifth Discipline Fieldbook: Strategies and Tools for Building and Learning Organization, p.242. 1994.

If we look at this Ladder of Inference, we see seven rungs. The first rung reminds us that there is an infinite amount of *observable data* out there that we could choose to notice about a person or situation. Some of us notice certain things over other things. I have a friend who could always spot a new piece of jewelry or hairstyle on someone, whereas, I confess to being oblivious to such details. So, we each, often quite unconsciously, *select data* out (rung two) from that observable data, and this is what we pay attention to (tattoos and boots). From there, we very quickly climb rungs three through six by adding *meaning* to what we're noticing—making *assumptions*, drawing *conclusions*, and adopting *beliefs* (This guy could be trouble. I have nothing in common with him). These in turn create some action on our part (ignoring my seatmate).

Remember that everything from rung two through six happens in our heads in a nanosecond. It's invisible to others. All people see is that something happens, resulting in our action. At times, though, things like air pockets and the conversation that followed bring new data into our awareness. This new information challenged my original assumptions and beliefs and resulted in a new action. In fact, I had a new appreciation for this seatmate of mine and happily engaged him in more discussion. It's been said that the difference between a flower and a weed is a judgment. In this case, that was true.

This cycle of judgment isn't always broken for us. New information isn't always brought so readily into our awareness. At times, we need to be responsible for our own ladder-climbing. We have the option to suspend this quick trip up the ladder to potentially faulty assumptions and inappropriate actions. But doing so means stepping back and being open to seeing things we don't initially see, letting new information in, testing the stories we make up, and then taking informed, conscious action.

What does this mean for you as a leader?

During times of change you're on your own trip, traveling between *what was* and *what will be*. On that journey, your thoughts inform your actions. And as a leader, your thoughts and actions send a ripple through the organization. So, it pays to understand the ladder I climbed to get from a thumbs-down to a thumbs-up about my seatmate on that plane. We can apply it in the workplace as well.

Let's look at some workplace examples:

Imagine that Bob shows up to a meeting late. In a few seconds flat, you can climb the ladder to some conclusion: he's casual about time, especially for meetings he doesn't value or for whose topics don't interest him, so it's unlikely he'll support what you are proposing at this meeting. Before you know it, you're getting defensive with Bob. And he has no clue why. Isn't it possible he was detained by a customer who needed his help?

Employees climb their ladders about leaders, too. Here's one I hear all the time, no matter the organization I work with. Susan passes a leader in the hallway and says hello. The leader doesn't respond. She adds meaning that he intentionally disregarded her. She assumes it's because of her status in the organization. He doesn't value people like her who are low on the org chart. She develops a belief that the leader is all about hierarchy. She chooses to share her story and opinion about this leader with anyone who will listen that day. What she may not have seen is that the leader had a Bluetooth on and was on a call. Or that he was distracted and rushing to a meeting he was late for. Or that he had just gotten some upsetting news from home and didn't even hear her greeting.

If leaders don't understand system dynamics, ladder climbing can lead to some wrong assumptions and bad moves. Most of the time, the story we make up is personal. We take things personally, that have nothing to do with us. What's happening is more about the organizational space we and others are in. Let's say you are a middle manager. Your boss is always telling the team that he welcomes good ideas for how to improve the operation. So, you send an email to him with an idea that you just know could make a great difference and even save the organization money. You grow excited to hear his reaction. But weeks go by with no acknowledgement. You climb your ladder. You conclude that he's not as sincere about wanting to solicit good ideas from the staff as he says. You happily share this conclusion with others. The fact is, your leader is negotiating an acquisition, preparing for a board meeting, and also dealing with some issues on the home front. Tops never seem to have enough time to manage all the responsibilities and complexity in their space. Relative to the rest of his work, your great idea is on the back burner. It isn't personal at all. Before you discourage others from sharing their ideas with the boss, you may want to collect some additional information by checking in with him.

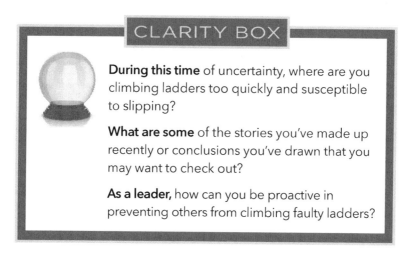

CLARITY BOX

During this time of uncertainty, where are you climbing ladders too quickly and susceptible to slipping?

What are some of the stories you've made up recently or conclusions you've drawn that you may want to check out?

As a leader, how can you be proactive in preventing others from climbing faulty ladders?

None of us has had to be trained in the art form of making up stories. We just do it. It makes us human. There's no need to beat yourself up about it. Just be mindful of it.

Under stress, we race up these ladders all day every day, potentially reaching all sorts of wrong conclusions and acting in ways that won't ultimately serve us or others well. As Mark Twain is credited for saying, "It ain't what you don't know that gets you into trouble. It's what you know for sure that just ain't so." Have you ever wished you could hit rewind and take something you said or did back after getting more data?

REFLECT ON WHAT YOU'RE THINKING

A professor of mine in grad school was known for saying, "Think about what you're thinking." That didn't make any sense to me until I met this Ladder of Inference model. Now I see the value of reflecting—of getting into the habit of noticing what I'm thinking, what assumptions I'm making, and what actions I may be unconsciously taking. If I remain open and am willing to test my assumptions, I often realize they aren't accurate or are built on incomplete information.

But during times of uncertainty, we crave certainty. So, out of our desire to make sense of things, we can be quick to make meaning out of what's happening.

What we pay attention to will dictate the meaning we make and then how we feel. We often overlook other data that could lead us to making a different meaning out of our circumstances and going down a different road.

Diane, a coaching client, was sent to me by her employer who believed she needed some support. He believed in Diane and didn't want to lose her from the team. When she first met me, she was very distraught. She shared the story of how her teammates didn't like her and didn't value her. She was sure her boss sent her to coaching because he thought she had issues and probably wanted to see her gone. She continued to spin the tale of a work world in collapse. By the end of her soliloquy, she had concluded that she might have to quit! *Whoa, what was going on here?*

I probed further and asked her how she knew those things. She had clear answers and examples and a definitive attitude about being right about her work situation. I knew otherwise, but didn't debate her.

Instead, I listened and then gave her a coaching assignment. I invited her to go back to her job for the next two weeks and tell herself a different story. This time I wanted her to *act as if* everyone on her team valued her and the job she did and that her boss respected her and wanted her to stay. She looked at me like I was crazy, which I kindly ignored, and we agreed to meet two weeks later.

When Diane showed up for our next coaching session, the first thing I noticed was a glow about her, long before she uttered a word. "Catch me up," I invited. "Tell me about these past two weeks."

She bubbled over, "They were amazing! I actually feel like my teammates might like me after all. I felt very valued by my boss. We had a great conversation about some of the things I need, and he's totally supportive. My interactions these past two weeks were great. I really can't believe the change."

Here's the irony, the only thing that had changed was the story Diane had chosen to tell herself, the data she was focusing on, and the assumptions she was making. When she changed her belief to include the possibility that others did regard her highly, the evidence showed up.

Diane and I discussed this odd phenomenon. Truth is, we get to be right about whatever story we make up because the evidence that we're right will appear. We're screening everything else out. If you tell yourself it's going to be a bad day, chances are you'll notice every bad thing that happens and will most certainly have a bad day. If you tell yourself you're going to have a great day, you'll likely notice all of the great things in the day. It's fun to be right. Which one would you rather be right about? Having a good day or a bad day? That life is conspiring against you and falling apart, or that life is in its own uncomfortable way falling together for you right now?

My next assignment for Diane was to choose. Did she want to be right about the story that she wasn't valued and should quit, or that she was valued and could stay? She chose the latter. She's still happily in place on that team years later and has been promoted more than once. When I'm onsite and see her in the hallways, she still lights up and reminisces about that session.

It can pay to reflect—to "think about what we're thinking." We can challenge the voice in our heads or at least notice what it's saying. Only then can we be open to a different possibility, other data, and a different story. It's important to check out our stories before we run too far down the field with them. Crazy as it sounds, we can create a big story in our head, complete with data and evidence. And before we know it we are a victim of some very bad situation and have made someone else out to be the villain. Or perhaps we're the hero of the story. They are the only two roles we tend to cast ourselves in.

MAKE YOUR THINKING KNOWN

Understanding the Ladder of Inference gives us the choice to do more reflecting on our thinking and on the stories we make up, since stories are at the root of most misunderstandings. *The other important avenue for avoiding misunderstanding is making our thinking clear to one another.* In the same way that we can't read others' minds, they can't read ours. So, it's up to us to be more transparent.

Sometimes we simply don't think about it, and we assume others know the "why" behind our thinking. Other times, we may feel vulnerable sharing what's on our minds. Either way, it's important to hone this skill or muster up the courage. Because when we don't make our thinking known, others make up their own stories about what we are thinking and doing.

This concept of "why" is so important. Whether leading at work or home, understanding "why" gives others less room for ladder climbing and making up untrue stories. Where there's an absence of information, people fill in the blanks. And they don't fill them in with positive information. They often fill it in with information far more negative than the reality. But we often don't think to fill in those blanks for others, or we don't think we have to.

We've all been on the frustrating receiving end of this, haven't we? Or am I the only one whose parents used to say, "Because I said so," as their answer to why I had to do something? Remember how that felt? It was crazy making, a show of dominance, and a discounting of my need to better understand all rolled into one.

Answering "why" is especially important during transitions. Even when others may not like the answer, they will feel respected. I encourage anyone leading a transition, whether you are leading your department through a reorganization or your children through a move, to explain "Why us? Why this? Why now?" When others are "let in on things" there are fewer blanks to fill in for themselves and less danger of them making up some very bad stories.

I've learned this lesson through my own leadership mistakes.

I was unknowingly made out to be a villain by one of my direct reports, Kelly. I had asked her to provide me with an activity report detailing the projects she was currently working on and an update on each. What I didn't realize was the story she made up about my request. By the time she provided me with the list, I could tell she was annoyed and angry. In a huff, she declared, "You're not the only one around here who's busy, Brenda. I may not make a big deal out of all the work I'm doing, but I have plenty of it. I don't need to be checked up on."

I was mystified by her reaction, which no doubt showed on my face. I inquired, "What are you talking about, Kelly? I know how busy you are."

"Then why are you questioning my work contributions?"

"I'm not," I replied. "It's just that when I go to the senior leadership meeting to represent our work, I want to be sure I'm representing your projects as well as mine, in order to give you the visibility you deserve."

Now, it was Kelly's turn to be flummoxed. "Oh. That's why you wanted the report?"

We were then able to talk about my intention—one that I hadn't done a very good job of making clear. That left Kelly's brain wide open to fill in the blanks and make up a story about the "why" of my request. The story she clearly made up was that I was "snoopervising" her. I told Kelly I wished she had doubled back to ask me the "why" behind my request since it was unclear to her. Either of us could have prevented an unnecessary climb up a ladder not worth climbing.

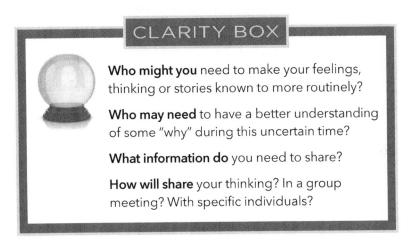

CLARITY BOX

Who might you need to make your feelings, thinking or stories known to more routinely?

Who may need to have a better understanding of some "why" during this uncertain time?

What information do you need to share?

How will share your thinking? In a group meeting? With specific individuals?

For years after that misunderstanding, we joked about it and used it as an example in the leadership training we facilitated. We practiced checking out our stories with one another and making our thinking known to each other. It wasn't unusual for a conversation to begin with one of us saying, "Here's the story I'm making up." It was an acknowledgement that it was a story. And it was an invitation for someone to challenge our assumptions or provide other information for our consideration. It became the basis of a very trusting and rich partnership.

In times of uncertainty, when clarity is already lacking, your clarity in communication has to be razor-sharp. No one can read your mind or know your intentions. You are the expert in that. How might you make it known? You may already be feeling vulnerable and reluctant to making your thoughts and feelings known, but it's especially important.

To head off a story you anticipate that someone will make up about your thinking or actions, try starting your conversation with openers like these:

* The reason I'm _____ is...

* Let me share my thinking with you.

* Here's the story I'm making up about what just happened.

* My intention is not _____; my intention is to _____.

* Here's why I'm doing this.

* I'm suggesting _____ because...

* Here's what I'm wondering about.

INQUIRE

In uncertain times, it's equally important to remember to inquire about what others are thinking, the ladders they're climbing, and the stories they are working with. If thought bubbles would appear over their heads, it would be so much easier. But in lieu of them, we need to make the effort. It's incumbent on us to uncover their whys, assumptions, and beliefs, rather than to jump to our own conclusions. It's important information to consider for decisions you may have to make. It may help you to know where you may need to clear up misunderstandings. And it creates a connection between you and others.

Leaders who spend as much time inquiring and listening as they do speaking and telling earn high regard from employees. People in general appreciate others taking an interest in understanding their thinking. They'll often be very happy to share. So long as you inquire respectfully and with a sincere curiosity to learn, it's appropriate. *How* you inquire, especially as a leader who is top to another staff member, is key. You don't want the other person to feel judged, attacked, or put on the spot. Your tone of voice will be key. There's the curious "why?" and the judgmental "why?" The only difference between them is in the delivery and the intention.

Here are some ways of moving conversations into inquiry mode:

* Help me to understand...

* Tell me about...

* What are you thinking about _____?

* What's the story you are making up about _____?

* Say more...

* How are you feeling?

* What's keeping you up at night?

* When you think about _____, what comes up for you?

When you catch yourself assuming something about someone else, especially in uncertain times, you could be projecting your thoughts onto them. Checking in with them and asking can help you course correct any assumptions you've made.

I saw this on a personal level when my family life was in transition. The time had come to sell what had been our family home for twelve years. I was having a hard time letting go emotionally. It was the house I had imagined being in forever, and I couldn't imagine vacating it. Just days before the move, I tucked my son into bed. My heart was heavy, and I imagined he was probably feeling equally distraught about the move to a simpler existence—a planned community that included the townhome we were about to call our new home. I wanted to be open with my son and give him the chance to process the change with me, too. So, I hesitantly approached the topic. It sounded something like, "Ya know, I'm feeling pretty sad about moving. So, I could imagine you are, too. If you are, it would be understandable, and it's okay. Do you want to talk about it?" His dry eyes met my wet eyes and he said, "Why would I be sad? I'm going to have a basketball court, pool, and tennis courts right in the neighborhood. I mean, what else could a kid want?" His genuine smile punctuated my inquiry.

We think we know what others are thinking, but it's likely we're making up a story or projecting our own "stuff" on them. I was so grateful I had inquired about my son's feelings. It lifted a burden I would have placed on myself, born of an assumption that I knew what was going on in his head.

Inquiry is its own magic. I've had more than one example of its magic effects and transformative powers.

Years ago I was hired to run a retreat between two departments of a client organization. They needed to bring the project managers together with the accounting team. Rumor was they "hated" each other. In fact, that disdain had been alive and well for years, and something finally had to be done about it.

After an entire day together, the root cause of their friction surfaced. It seemed that the project managers would send paperwork to the accounting department, who would use it to create client invoices. The accounting department required that changes be made in red ink. The project managers routinely disregarded this guideline and used blue or black ink. The accounting department would then send it back with a note that it was unacceptable unless presented in red ink. This would infuriate the project managers. And ultimately, the billing for clients would be delayed while they engaged in their standoff. That affected cash flow in the organization.

At the end of the retreat day, this issue finally surfaced. The project managers thought the accounting department was being "stupid" applying such randomness to the billing process. The accounting department thought the project managers were being intentionally difficult by not cooperating. The discussion got rather heated.

As facilitator, I stepped in and invited each side to answer one question: *why?* Accounting explained that the blue or black ink blended in with the print on the document. So, they often didn't see important billing information and were likely to make costly billing errors. The red ink jumped off the page and ensured greater accuracy in billing. They reminded the project managers that billing discrepancies only aggravated the client, and the project managers were then left to deal with this client service issue.

When I asked the project managers why they weren't complying with the request to use red ink, they simply answered, "We didn't understand why that was important. It seemed like a random request and show of power." As they discussed the issue, it quickly dissolved.

When they uncovered the "why's" of the situation, it actually made sense. The energy in the room immediately lightened and shifted to one of camaraderie. Team members gushed at my performance. Honestly, to this day, I remember feeling embarrassed that they saw me as so skilled. All I did was use one small word—"why?" Left unanswered, though, it leads to nothing but misunderstanding.

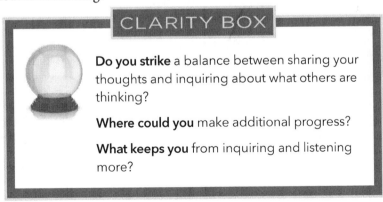

CLARITY BOX

Do you strike a balance between sharing your thoughts and inquiring about what others are thinking?

Where could you make additional progress?

What keeps you from inquiring and listening more?

During times of change and uncertainty the need for effective communication is critical. Inquiry paves the way for understanding—whether it's with your family member, friend, or colleagues at work. "Why?" is a powerful one-word tool that can shed light on unclear situations in order to see them for what they are. The information you uncover could become very valuable in helping you through transition fog and figuring out what you may need to do next. Your "next right things" will be built on clear understanding, rather than assumptions.

REFRAME!

Thinking about what you're thinking sometimes requires us to do something called reframing!

When "stuff happens" and we find ourselves in some plan B, it usually feels more like it's happening *to* us than *for* us. Only with time can we see that it was really in our best interest—that during the transition we're in, some big reshuffling of the deck is occurring. And while we might never want to go through it again, it's creating a necessary shift.

I won't pretend that the shifts I've experienced have always been much fun or that I always jump out of bed eager to embrace what's next. But I have noted the unexpected gifts in each of those shifts once I look at them in the rearview mirror. Knowing that the gifts are there, but may be temporarily out of view, has helped me to assume they are there even during uncertain times.

The skill that has served me best is called reframing. Wikipedia defines cognitive reframing as "a way of viewing and experiencing events, ideas, concepts, and emotions to find more positive alternatives."[9] In other words, it's being mindful of the ladder I'm climbing, of the story I'm making up at the time. And then it's choosing a different story. At times when I feel like I don't have much control over circumstances, the one thing I can control is my thoughts and the story I will choose.

For years, I've reframed parking challenges. I don't think or say, "I'll never find a spot." Instead, I've claimed something I call parking karma. Wherever we go, I say, "Now, where's my great parking spot?" And that spot almost always appears, right up front. My family has made jabs about this for years, but they've finally stopped. Because even in the rush of holiday mall or New York City parking, my spot is always there. They've grown used to my singing "parking karma" as I pull into my spot. I figure I can choose to see the glass as half-full or half-empty. And in uncertain times, we don't really know what will show up and where the shifts will ultimately take us. Just maybe they will lead us somewhere equally good or better. What's the harm in believing that?

How are you thinking about your situation? Perhaps it's some complex time in your organization that you need to lead others through. Perhaps it's a heartache or a health scare. The unknown is dark and scary. The switch that can turn that darkness into light though is reframing.

I still recall a pivotal phone conversation I had with my colleague, Andy, when my life was on its detour. He said, "Brenda, look at this time as a bridge. That's it. Simply a bridge to somewhere you can't see yet. Think about it that way." And that coaching helped me to reframe my return to corporate life again, at least temporarily. Thinking of it that way helped me to relax into the change and to make it a positive experience. I chose to see myself being called to a place that I needed during my transition and who needed me, too. Once I accepted this new reality, I became grateful. I met wonderful people, got to do good work, found a place to belong while feeling displaced in my personal life, and found meaning in the new situation.

You can reframe:

* A problem as an opportunity

* A weakness as a strength

* An impossibility as a distant possibility

* A distant possibility as a near possibility

* Unkindness as lack of understanding

I'm not suggesting magical thinking as an answer to uncertainty. I am, however, suggesting that a good reframe will clear the way for your next right moves to become clearer. They are easier to ascertain with a clearer, more possibility-laden approach. As author and psychologist Daniel Goleman writes in *A Force for Good*, "The stories we tell ourselves set limits or possibilities."[10]

So, consider *your* reframe:

* Have you lost a job OR received an opportunity to reevaluate your career options?

* Are you losing your child to college OR on the threshold of watching a young adult emerge in your life as a result of your parental job well done?

* Are the corporate budget cutbacks a nightmare OR an opportunity for the organization to explore efficiencies?

* Did you get dumped OR did you outgrow a relationship and gain the freedom to learn from this relationship and begin again?

* Is this organization transition the end of something good OR the beginning of something better?

I still remember a story I once heard on the radio. The host painted the picture of a guy who stood in front of a closed door, full of padlocks, lamenting his luck. He pounded hard on that door for a good long time. Longer than he should have. Eventually, he gave up and stepped back from the door, accepting defeat. When he did, he noticed that to the left and right of him were doors that had been there all along—doors with no locks, that were slightly ajar, and that were easy to walk through. But he was too busy trying to break down a door that had closed to see the amazing options to the left and right of him.

May you choose to reframe this time of uncertainty as a door of possibility yet to be opened. What will come of it is TBD.

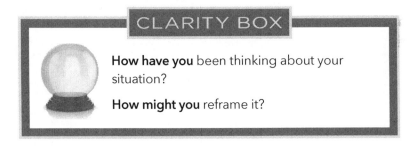

CLARITY BOX

How have you been thinking about your situation?

How might you reframe it?

MASTERING PLAN "BE"

✤ Reflect on the assumptions you are making. They will trigger your actions.

✤ Check the stories you make up. You often get to be right about the stories, whether they're good or bad.

✤ Seek to better understand what others are thinking. Don't assume you already know.

✤ Remember the power of sharing and communicating "why?"

✤ Make your thinking known to others. Don't assume they understand what's going on in your head or your intention.

✤ Reframe problems as more positive alternatives (problems could be opportunities).

CHAPTER 6

BE TOTALLY RESPONSE-ABLE

*"I am not a product of my circumstances.
I am a product of my decisions."*
—Stephen Covey

D URING TRANSITIONS WE often get tested. When I found myself unexpectedly taking over Pat's role as manager in my first corporate experience, it came with the inevitable top space responsibility and complexity. I was learning about the job, the industry, the organization, and the team. I was drinking from the proverbial fire hose. But it got turned on full force when I began to meet with the leaders in the organization who were our internal clients.

It appeared that in the wake of Pat's hard-charging approach and disdain for political correctness there were some connections to make and bridges to mend. And so, that's what led me to Akram's wood-paneled office. I needed to hear what our internal clients most wanted and expected from our department.

Akram was a key leader in the organization. He was a big man, but his reputation as an emotional, outspoken, and intimidating guy was even bigger. So, I straightened to my full five-foot-tall height and tried not to look surprised when I found not one, but two stern-faced men awaiting me. Akram had also invited his right-hand man, John. And they had an axe to grind.

I flipped open my leather portfolio ready to bond and take notes on how I could best partner with them. They had other ideas. They wanted to vent their frustration about the past with someone. And it appeared, I was that someone. They raged on—one thunder, the other lightning. The flash and fury in quick succession. And I was feeling like I had been left standing in a field holding an umbrella, a lightning rod that my predecessor had handed me on her way out the door.

I was here to explore the blue skies of tomorrow. They were not. Hard as I tried to reroute that conversation, the storm continued.

Now, even in my twenties, I wasn't willing to play victim, so I did what was natural for me and stunning to them. I quietly closed my portfolio, stood up, and politely stated, "I'm sorry for the dissatisfaction you've had with our department in the past. I came here to discuss how to move forward and ensure it doesn't happen again. But you don't seem ready to have that conversation. So, I'm going to go now. Please call me when and if you are ready to have that conversation."

And I left the room.

As I was putting on my coat, I heard some movement behind me. It was Akram. He had caught up to me in the hallway. He appeared a tad sheepish and lured me back to his office with the promise that they would "behave." And while their behavior was improved, it wasn't stellar. But we muddled through a conversation.

When I returned to my office in the building across the street, my phone was ringing. I picked up and rattled off my greeting. But before I could finish it, I heard a booming voice say "Brenda? This is Akram." Pause. "We are going to be fine, you and me. Just fine. You told me what I needed to hear. I respect that. I will behave better."

Now, I doubt Akram had *ever* been confronted on his behavior before, let alone by a newly hired, miniature, ex-junior high school English teacher. But he underestimated how even a few years of teaching crazed eighth and ninth graders had prepared me for the corporate world. And the truth is, we went on to be easy partners in my time there. We still have an occasional lunch together.

GIVE UP FAULT. PRODUCE RESULTS.

In times of complexity and especially in unwelcome transitions, have you ever noticed that we need to figure out what went wrong and who is to blame? After being passed up for a promotion, when the project goes south, after a breakup, after discovering a flat tire, we want to know the source of the problem and where to lay blame. It's our human default. Was it me? Or was it them?

But fault and blame are distractors. What if we agree that while you and I aren't to *blame* for what's happened, we certainly are responsible!

Yes, that's what I said. We…are…responsible.

But, wait. I was clearly *not responsible* for anything that had happened before I came into that new leadership role. And I was *not responsible* for the fact that these two men acted out, right? And you may be sputtering right now that you aren't responsible for your flat tire, your health issue, getting laid off, or whatever your struggle is, right?

That may depend on your definition of the word. What comes to mind when you hear the word *responsible*?

Fault? It wasn't your fault, right? It's like getting stuck in traffic. It isn't your fault there's a traffic jam on the highway. But it does elicit feelings. What do *you* do? Do you rant? Fume? Pound the steering wheel? Use hand gestures? Take it out on your passengers? Blame the idiot who just *had* to have his car breakdown at the exact time you were trying to get to dinner in the city? (I love this particular reaction. As though the guy decided it would be fun to get stranded along the highway just to mess with your day. Sounds crazy, huh?) But our human nature does produce these types of emotional reactions, and our emotions obscure just how responsible we really are.

That's right. In the end we *are* responsible. Understanding this is key to seeing our uncertain situation differently and helping us to feel empowered. I learned this years ago from my long-time mentor, Dr. Michael Durst, a pioneer in the application of internal locus of control in the workplace and author of *Napkin Notes: On the Art of Living.*[11] Michael delivered some impactful training called Management by Responsibility for the organization where I was Training Manager. He had a special way of exploring the concept of excellence.

We used to think the key factors related to excellent performance or desirable outcomes were **potential, desire**, and **knowledge**. We now know that none of these—potential, desire, or knowledge—is the key factor for excellence. There is one other factor that is much more important.

To illustrate this, let me ask you a few questions:

How many of you would like to be at your ideal weight and physically fit? (Most hands typically fly up. Feel free to raise yours even if I can't see it. Mine is right there with you.)

Seems there's a lot of *DESIRE* here.

How many of you have the *POTENTIAL* to be at your ideal weight and physically fit?

Of course you do! Me, too!

How many of you have the *KNOWLEDGE*? Do you know what it would take to be at your ideal weight and physically fit? Kinds of foods to eat, not eat, importance of exercise? C'mon now, be honest. Sure we do! Say no to donuts and yes to broccoli, right? Say yes to a walk and no to the TV remote. Great, we have the knowledge!

Here's the kicker: how many of us *are* at our ideal weight and physically fit? Something tells me a lot of hands just went down. Mine, too.

So, the question is, why not? We have some key ingredients—potential, desire, and knowledge. But the number one ingredient, the key to excellence, is missing. It's *responsibility.*

Responsibility is a willingness to do what it takes to produce the results. Are we willing to do what it takes to produce the results? Are we willing to take one hundred percent responsibility? That's the real question. Are we willing to pass up the donuts in the break room? Are we willing to hit the gym after a long day? Oh, and by the way, giving 50 percent won't produce the results. Responsibility comes in only one real denomination: 100 percent.

Don't worry. We know how to take 100 percent responsibility. It's when things are going well that we are most likely to take responsibility—100 percent, in fact. We take credit, full accountability. We assume our efforts are paying off. We see ourselves as the source of the good things happening to us. The promotion, the pay raise, the well-deserved vacation.

We do it unconsciously. Think back to being in school. When you brought that A home, what did you say to your parents? "I got an A." You were happy to take responsibility.

When you brought the D home, what did you say? "*She* gave me a D." Notice what happens when things aren't going well. We take 0 percent of the responsibility and accountability. We revert to blame. We assume no control, as though that teacher sat at the kitchen table, wrote that subpar paper herself, and put our name on it.

I recently had a coaching session with a leader who had not produced the results his executive was looking for on a project. When confronted by his executive, this leader began to discuss his team and how they hadn't done what they should have. He expressed his disappointment in them. The executive was not happy with that response. But his frustration wasn't with the team, it was with this leader. He didn't want to hear how it was someone else's fault. He wanted to hear his direct report take full responsibility for the results and then describe what he was going to do next.

No matter what's going on, the one thing we have total control over is how we respond. Our *ability* to manage our *response* consciously. Our response–ability. It's not really about what happens. It's not about why it happened or who's to blame. It's more about what to do or how *to be* with what happens. It's about your ability to choose your response to it.

That isn't to say we don't react with some emotion when the unexpected shows up. Anger at the traffic. Frustration at how the meeting's going. Distress over being laid off. Kicking the flat tire. Lamenting that life isn't giving us what we expected. We're human.

So, we need to feel those feelings, but then get on with it. Holding on to the negative emotions won't really accomplish anything except making ourselves and others miserable. Replaying where it went wrong and whose fault it is won't help a thing either. In fact, it will only thicken your transition fog. But since you're human, get your reaction out of the way. That way you can create some emotional distance from the event to do the only thing you can do, the next right thing: make some **choices**.

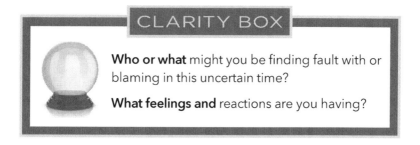

CLARITY BOX

Who or what might you be finding fault with or blaming in this uncertain time?

What feelings and reactions are you having?

THE POWER TO CHOOSE

It's in the choice that you find power—the power to choose your reaction to whatever is going on around you. It's better than falling prey to an unconscious knee-jerk reaction or assuming you have no choice. Take comfort that you do have options.

When foggy situations show up, at home or work, you have three clear response-able choices, often in this order:

1. Change/influence it.

2. Accept it.

3. Get out of it.

I like knowing I don't have to be a victim of any situation. It's the glass-half-full awareness that no matter what happens, no matter how uncertain times are, we always have control over one thing—how we respond. To quote Maya Angelou, "You may not control all the events that happen to you, but you can decide not to be reduced by them."

In most cases, I start with trying to influence the situation or to create a change. I didn't have much luck with that in round one of my adversarial meeting with Akram and John. So, option two was up. Could I accept this treatment? And by accept, I mean accept it and not complain or play martyr later. The answer was no. I had accepted as much as I was willing to temporarily. So, I chose to get out of the situation.

Knowing I always have these options makes me feel powerful, even in tough situations. Ideally, it will help you to think through situations that come your way, too. And it will help others see that they also have choices. Otherwise, we get stuck in victim mode—seeing no options and growing resentful.

I'm not suggesting the options will necessarily be easy to act on, but they are options. We can choose to be stuck or to move on, even if moving on means moving on in our minds and accepting a situation, at least for now. We can rant at the traffic. Or we can accept that no amount of cursing will move that traffic any faster, and we can tune in to a favorite radio station. We can kick that flat tire and spend the rest of the week being miserable. Or we can have our outburst and then accept the circumstances. Either way the outcome is the same: we need to get it repaired. Period. End of story. Why not get busy moving on, figuring out what to do with the situation faster, and getting it behind us?

The best example of choosing to respond to bad news and accept something that couldn't be changed or influenced came from my master-in-reframing, Yoda-like son. He has always been my teacher. I watch him respond to change, disappointments, and unexpected news time and again. But this particular example may be just what you need to remember as you navigate some foggy times.

The day his dad and I shared that we were going our separate ways, my son retreated to the basement to lose himself in a video game. I let some time pass and then went down to check in on him. "I'm sure that wasn't exactly what you wanted to hear today," I stammered.

He shrugged his little six-year-old shoulders, looked at me, and simply stated, "It is what it is, Mom. But it doesn't *have* to be bad."

There was really nothing else left to be said. Even at a time of significant change, he exercised power—his power to choose. He made a choice to accept what was happening and reframe it as something that didn't have to be bad. His reaction and that statement carries me through transition fog to this day. Because he was right. It doesn't *have* to be bad. I offer that up to you now. Perhaps you can see your time of change as something that doesn't have to be bad.

I know from experience that we don't just sail through these options, depending on the magnitude of the situation. We could spend years trying to influence or change something to no avail. And then accept it to the best of our ability, at least temporarily. And then determine we need to move on. So, I don't present these options lightly or mean to imply they are easy. We can exercise them quickly in some situations, but we require much more time and effort in other situations. Knowing we have them keeps us from getting stuck in *what was* or *how it should be*. It keeps us moving on, knowing we're consciously exercising our choices.

What situation do you know you need to take more responseability for? Perhaps you are stuck or feeling like a victim. Perhaps you find yourself spending more time complaining or feeling guilty about circumstances than doing anything about them. The truth may be that you simply aren't willing to do what it takes to produce the results—like speaking up to your boss or losing that ten pounds. But if you really aren't willing to do what it takes to change the situation, you may have to accept circumstances for what they are…at least for now. Accept it. Or choose a different response.

Fill in the blanks to the following statements:

* **One area of my life or one situation that I have not felt responsible for is...**
* **So I've reacted by...**
* **A better response might be...**

How might you put this three-choice approach to responsibility into practice for yourself and as a leader coaching others? Try presenting these options in your coaching conversations with others. Be a leader who gently reminds others that they have choices in how they react to situations. These choices are our power during times when we feel otherwise powerless.

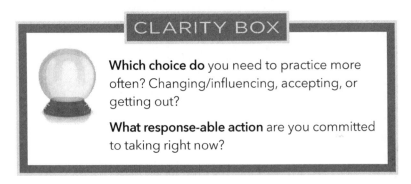

CLARITY BOX

Which choice do you need to practice more often? Changing/influencing, accepting, or getting out?

What response-able action are you committed to taking right now?

THE MOST IMPORTANT CHOICE OF ALL IN UNCERTAIN TIMES

We'd all prefer guarantees and total control in uncertain times. But they don't exist. Let's face it, the clarity that follows an uncertain time is quickly replaced by the next uncertain time. It's a cycle we experience in the workplace and in life in general.

So, we ultimately need to embrace uncertainty and learn how to *be* with it.

Will you hope that it all works out and fear that it won't?

Or will you choose to see it as something that is already working out and accept the wonder of that?

When we replace our *fear* of uncertainty with *wonder* and *curiosity* about what's unfolding, *"now what's?"* become *"why not's?"*

I concur with Susan Jeffers, author of *Embracing Uncertainty*, who writes "all of life's creativity flourishes not in certainty, but in the questions that flow from uncertainty."[12]

I urge you to take a childlike approach to change. Instead of hoping everything will be all right, choose to see that it already is. See it through the lens of awe and wonderment. Children don't hurry from place to place. They take their time. They see all there is to see. They accept what is. Even when a sunny day turns to rain, they have an uncanny ability to find the fun in getting wet or jumping in puddles. Their "now what" becomes a "why not?" They choose to see the shift in weather with awe and wonder. It's an adventure.

I urge you to embrace your uncertainty with wonder.

I wonder how this will all turn out.
I wonder what this is going to make possible.
I wonder what I'm going to do about this.
I wonder what good is going to come from this.
I wonder what I will learn from this.

Choose to be an adventurer rather than a worrier. When you do, uncertainty can be reframed as an exciting opportunity. And you'll get others in the workplace more routinely asking "why not?" than "now what?" on the way to great possibilities.

MASTERING PLAN "BE"

✤ Remember lesson #1–plan A is an illusion, get ready to act *response-ably* during plan B.

✤ Be human. Have your emotional reaction, but don't let it drag on.

✤ Refuse to play the fault/blame game when things aren't perfect. Ask yourself, "What will I choose now?"

✤ Change what is in your power or try to influence what isn't.

✤ Accept the situation–at least for now. Truly accepting means no whining.

✤ Get out of the situation–in whatever big or small ways are appropriate. (This could be as simple as walking away from a dispute or as big as walking away from a job opportunity that isn't right for you.)

✤ Ask yourself, "Am I willing to do what it takes to produce the desired results?"

✤ Approach uncertainty with curiosity over fear. Choose to be an adventurer rather than a worrier.

CHAPTER 7

BE OPEN TO FEEDBACK— WHAT YOU DO WITH IT IS UP TO YOU

"What receivers do with feedback is totally within their control. They can reject all of it, or any part of it, swallow it whole or spit it out, distort it, adore it, hate it, forget it, or remember it forever."
—Edie Seashore

As a leader you are probably no stranger to feedback—both giving it and receiving it. It's unavoidable in the leadership space and comes in many forms: informal sharing in the hallway, performance discussions, and coaching sessions, to name a few. It can be delivered directly to you, through a third party, or via assessments on everything from your personality style to how your team perceives your leadership.

In times of change or uncertainty, you may especially find yourself searching for answers. So, you seek out others' opinions and feedback. Then again, in this time of uncertainty, you may simply be on the receiving end of a lot of unsolicited feedback from others. Lucky you.

They say feedback is a gift. And while it can be, it doesn't always feel that way. And knowing what to do with the feedback can be its own challenge, especially if you get a lot of conflicting feedback that just contributes to your transition fog. That can be quite confusing.

I attended an off-site retreat years ago. After receiving some confounding feedback from some other attendees, I found myself in an all-out tailspin. Edie Seashore, pioneer in the field of organization development, and co-author of *What Did You Say? The Art of Giving and Receiving Feedback*,[13] just so happened to be on the scene as the retreat facilitator. She witnessed my distress and acted. That's a nice way of saying that this refined and impeccably-dressed woman who was never without a strand of pearls around her neck, grabbed me by the neck, pulled me into a private space, and inquired, "What the hell happened to you?"

As I sniffled my way through my experience, she coached me to remember that what I did with the feedback I had gotten was entirely up to me. I could "reject all of it, or any part of it, swallow it whole or spit it out, distort it, adore it, hate it, forget it, or remember it forever."[14]

At the time, that seemed like a revelation. I didn't have to blindly accept. I hope that gives you the same freedom and power that it has me where receiving feedback is concerned. We get to *choose* what to do with feedback. The feedback may be accurate, but then again it may not be. You can assess for yourself how, or if, you're going to act on it. This awareness is a reframe that feels like a superpower I have to use when facing feedback—especially in uncertain times when I'm foggy enough already.

Remembering that it's up to the receiver of feedback to do what they will with it has also lifted a burden for me in my love/hate relationship with providing feedback to others. As feedback givers, our role is to provide our perspective appropriately, maintaining the receiver's self-esteem in the process. But what the receiver ultimately does with that feedback is entirely up to them. We can't really make anyone do anything with it. Whether I'm coaching and providing feedback, helping someone process feedback they've received, or receiving it myself, this awareness has liberated me from feedback fear. I hope it will do the same for you.

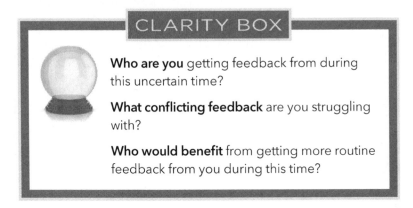

CLARITY BOX

Who are you getting feedback from during this uncertain time?

What conflicting feedback are you struggling with?

Who would benefit from getting more routine feedback from you during this time?

DEFINING FEEDBACK

The term "feedback" plays a special role in aeronautics and is often linked to that industry. In flying from point A to point B, it's said that airplanes are off-course over 90 percent of the time. That's a bit scary for those of us who spend far too much time on airplanes, right? Thanks to the feedback on the instrumentation panel, however, pilots can make continual course corrections and get us to our destination, despite headwinds, downdrafts, and other unexpected turbulence. That makes feedback a pretty useful tool, wouldn't you agree? Yet, most of us don't leap out of bed in the morning, excited about the feedback we'll be delivering or receiving that day.

In its pure sense, feedback isn't positive or negative. It's just data. But we all have different reactions to the word "feedback" based on our experiences of it. Over our lifetime we've gotten feedback from our parents, family, teachers, bosses, work colleagues, and friends. Some of it has been very helpful and some of it has been hurtful. So, as humans, we assign feedback a value. We talk about it as negative or positive.

But in and of itself, feedback is simply information.

* **Feedback can be information about the gap between expected results and actual results**. This is the gap between what's expected and what's actually happening. For example, if you hold an 8:30 a.m. project meeting every Wednesday, but it typically doesn't begin until 8:40 a.m., you may get some feedback about your meetings not starting on time.

* **Feedback can be information about the impact your actions are having on others. It's like having someone hold up a mirror for you.** As you're trying to figure things out and lead the way during complex, confusing times, you may be sending mixed signals or doing things that have a negative impact on others. Feedback helps you become aware of these unintended consequences. Feedback is about what you're doing, not what you are intending. For example, you may be having difficulty figuring out the next best strategic move. You take your time, carefully analyzing this decision. What you don't realize is how frustrated others are waiting for your guidance and direction so they can get on with their work. Their feedback can bring that into focus for you.

You will always be the expert on your intention—no one but you knows your intention. However, others are the experts on your impact—only they know the impact of your actions. Feedback can help you to get in touch with your impact on others during this time of uncertainty. It can provide some helpful clarity.

We could say that feedback *feels negative* when the message is discouraging our behaviors by communicating that our behaviors didn't have the intended effects. It implies we may want to change something about our behavior. Perhaps your day got crazy and you decided to move a scheduled performance review conversation with a staff member to another day. Your intent was to move it into a day when you could be more focused, but your direct report shares that it made him feel like his performance discussion wasn't a priority for you.

It *feels positive* when the feedback is information that reinforces behaviors and encourages repetition of those behaviors by communicating that they had the intended, desired effects. Perhaps you are sending out routine updates on the changes your organization is experiencing and receiving real appreciation for keeping everyone informed. This fuels you to continue those updates.

Mostly, feedback is food for thought, and if delivered well, should be easily digestible.

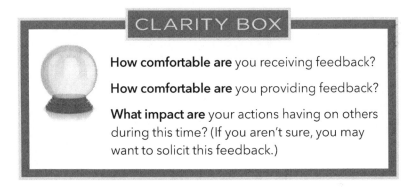

CLARITY BOX

How comfortable are you receiving feedback?

How comfortable are you providing feedback?

What impact are your actions having on others during this time? (If you aren't sure, you may want to solicit this feedback.)

SWALLOWING FEEDBACK WHOLE OR SPITTING IT OUT

Uncertainty attracts feedback or sends us scrambling for some.

If you've ever talked about your uncertainty over an upcoming medical procedure, you know exactly what I mean. Suddenly, everyone wants to tell you their stories (often horror stories) and provide you with more medical advice than you bargained for. Or you mention your upcoming vacation to Italy and uncertainty over where to go, and suddenly, everyone is a tour guide, telling you where to go and what you "just have to do." Mention you're between jobs, and the world will inundate you with well-intended advice and feedback.

We think we want feedback—until we get it. It can provide clarity or add to our confusion.

The big question is, what feedback should you listen to and what should you reject?

Go ahead, listen to others. But keep in mind that their opinions and feedback will reflect their own conditioning and experiences. The colleague who's been with the company for twenty-five years will have a different perspective than the new hire. The person who loved visiting Pompeii will have far different feedback and advice for you than the person who hated it. I have friends who raved about Pompeii. I, on the other hand, couldn't get out of Pompeii fast enough. Your Uber driver may have a different take on what to do while you're between jobs than your spouse. This inconsistent feedback can be tricky to process.

I once solicited feedback on a big and visible project I was working on that had the power to alter my career. I reached out to some professionals that I knew I could count on for great guidance. But in the end, they each gave me drastically different feedback that didn't match up. I thought their feedback would help me make great progress. Instead, it brought me to a screeching halt. The monkey chatter in my brain went into overdrive, ruminating over the conflicting feedback. That part of me that expected clarity and got confusion pitched a fit. What should I do? Who should I listen to? Now what?

I realized that when I solicited feedback, people really wanted to help out and contribute. So, they find feedback and offer their opinions. But sometimes, they aren't really the experts on whatever you're asking them about. So, keep in mind that not everyone's feedback will be equally valuable or worthy of your consideration.

In fact, at times you know best! I realized that if only I could get quiet, the swirl of my thoughts would settle to the bottom like sand in a glass of water, and I'd see more clearly. So, I talked it out, took a walk, gave myself permission to just *be* and not *do* anything right away. That involved a highly evolved form of meditation you may be familiar with. I flopped myself on the couch and watched hours of upbeat television shows involving singing and dancing. It helped me hit the reset button on myself. And I got a good night's rest.

The next day, with a quieter mind, I began to get clearer. *My* voice took over. I could hear it, like a trumpet heralding some welcome clarity.

When confronted with conflicting feedback, listen to what your gut is telling you. What feels right to you and what doesn't feel right to you is important data, too.

During my divorce, I remember a friend who always reminded me, "Just because someone says it, doesn't make it true." That's right. I knew I needed to listen to my colleagues' feedback, then step back, determine whose feedback I may need to disqualify based on their conditioning, factor in my own opinion, and choose how to move forward.

In the end, we're the ones who need to decide and deal with the consequences of our choices. Often, no one else can tell us what to do or know better than we can. After all, only you know if you want to visit the cities of Italy, the wine country, or the scenic Amalfi coast. If you want to see the Pope, people watch at an outdoor café, or sign up for a cooking class.

How often have you found yourself in a similar bind? Maybe you had some 360-degree feedback delivered to you, and you tried to make sense of it. Your boss scored you high, but your peers didn't. Or perhaps your team loved an idea, and your boss hated it. Or your spouse gushed over your wardrobe choice while your kids rolled their eyes.

In uncertainty, we're likely to seek feedback. Or we're likely to get inundated with it even when we aren't seeking it. Everyone will want to help and offer input. And that's okay. You simply need to know how to sort through it.

Here are some key questions to ask yourself as you figure out which feedback to swallow whole and which feedback to spit out.

* Whose feedback should I immediately disqualify based on their conditioning or some bias they may have?

* Who is especially qualified to give me feedback in this situation? Who isn't?

* If I were to stop trying to please everyone, what would I do?

* If I valued my own opinion as much as I do others', what would I do?

* When I still my mind, what does some part of me know I should do?

* If this is a misstep, how will I recalculate?

You don't have to act on every piece of feedback you get. You do, however, need to become a master of discernment.

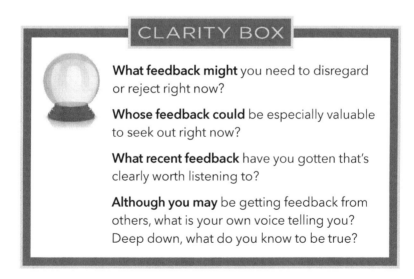

CLARITY BOX

What feedback might you need to disregard or reject right now?

Whose feedback could be especially valuable to seek out right now?

What recent feedback have you gotten that's clearly worth listening to?

Although you may be getting feedback from others, what is your own voice telling you? Deep down, what do you know to be true?

DISTORTIONS AND BLIND SPOTS

We can't see ourselves as others see us. So, feedback really can be a gift if we are open to it. It sheds light on things that are otherwise in our blind spot and brings information into our awareness.

One of the craziest activities I've had teams do during retreats is to tape a big piece of flipchart paper on their backs. They then take turns writing words or phrases to describe each person on the papers. Naturally, it's positive feedback. I then invite them to have a seat while we talk about the topic of feedback. Meanwhile, they are burning with curiosity about the words on their backs. Words that others have seen before them. They become the last ones to know what others have said.

It's rather symbolic, wouldn't you say? How often do people talk behind each other's backs instead of providing feedback directly? That is so often the case. We are the last ones to know about our impact.

After keeping the participants in the dark for a while, I invite them to take the feedback sheets off their backs. The energy that gets unleashed in the room at the unveiling of this feedback, and the emotion in the eyes and faces of the recipients, is always powerful. They giggle, smile broadly, ooh and ah. It's a statement about how little feedback we get from those we work with. Perhaps most indicative of the power of feedback is how gingerly each participant folds this feedback sheet and tucks it away. Years later, I've crossed paths with participants who admit to still having it stashed away in some special place.

Feedback, even when constructive, is attention. Providing it lets our employees know they matter to us, lets our kids know we care, and lets whoever the recipient is feel valued.

Those who provide it to us, do the same. We often need colleagues, friends, or family members to hold up a mirror for us. It brings into the light the things we just can't see about ourselves—the positives and the blind spots—so that we can grow from that awareness.

In times of transition, stress, and confusion, feedback can be incredibly valuable in helping us make course corrections that we couldn't even see as options. I owe a colleague's unsolicited feedback for one of the most important transitions of my life.

Remember the boss with the red marker who limited my interactions in the organization I was working for? Well, when she first joined the company, I had never met anyone I couldn't work with. And I was determined to find a way.

So, I enrolled in a week-long leadership program hosted by a world-class organization. I spent the week with a small group of other professionals sharing and learning. I confided my dilemma and sought feedback on what else I could be doing to smooth over this challenging workplace relationship with my boss.

Partway through that week, one of the facilitators, Jan, pulled me aside. She asked if I was open to some feedback. When I nodded yes, she continued, "Have you ever considered that nothing you do will make a difference in this relationship?" I was puzzled. What was she saying? That I was a failure?

"It seems your new boss may want you out of the way. She doesn't want it to work. So, it's possible nothing you do will make a difference."

As a still naïve young leader, I was stunned. This was clearly in my blind spot. It never occurred to me that someone wouldn't want a working relationship to succeed.

"Have you ever considered consulting?" she asked.

I went on to give her all the reasons why I couldn't do that—from the degrees I needed to my age. She had a counterpoint and suggestion for each objection I raised.

Flash forward—that moment of unsolicited feedback gave me the confidence to get out of the situation and start my own consulting practice when my work scenario grew even more complicated.

Never in a million years would I have considered that I couldn't make things work with my boss. Never ever would I have considered launching a consulting practice. Jan's feedback shed light on the situation and the options that I had been blind to. She clarified for me that I had tried to influence the situation with no luck, couldn't accept it as it was, and needed to get out of it. This feedback and decision not only changed the trajectory of my career, but the trajectory of my life. It's how BKR Consulting was born.

In uncertain times, it's helpful to surround yourself with truth-tellers. These may be people who are removed from the situation and can see it clearly, or they may be people closer to the situation who are willing to shed light on something you need to see.

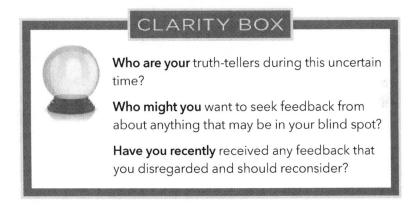

CLARITY BOX

Who are your truth-tellers during this uncertain time?

Who might you want to seek feedback from about anything that may be in your blind spot?

Have you recently received any feedback that you disregarded and should reconsider?

HATING IT

When someone starts a conversation with you by saying, "Are you open to some feedback?" what do you do? Cringe? Me, too. Why is that? For starters, personal experience probably left us with negative feelings about feedback. Teachers, parents, coaches, or bosses didn't use it well. It was painful and left us feeling inadequate, or worse.

Here are some feedback traps to avoid and some tips for delivering feedback that others can swallow. These factors impact why we and others may hate or resist feedback.

It's poorly timed.

Have you ever had someone chime in with some "helpful feedback" when you were coming unglued? It's less than ideal to give or get feedback when either the giver or receiver is feeling emotional. If you've ever tried to provide feedback to your son or daughter on the heels of their sporting event, you know what I mean. Timing is everything. And emotional time-outs can be in order. The only feedback I provide on that car ride home from a lacrosse game, no matter the outcome, is simply, "I love watching you play."

It's exaggerated.

Try telling someone on your staff that they are *always* late to meetings and watch what happens. Or tell your boss that he *never* comes out of his office. See what happens. Using superlatives like *always* and *never* start debates. Or shut us down. Once you've experienced enough plan B's, you realize words like *always* and *never* should be used infrequently. Tentative language actually works better to keep the dialogue going and makes feedback more palatable: "You *might* want to consider circulating among the staff more routinely." Or, "You *may* need to leave earlier to get to our meetings on time."

It isn't specific enough.

I once had a performance review where my manager started every sentence with "I have a sense that…" It became clear and almost laughable that she really wasn't tuned in to my performance at all. I left that review with no idea if I was being fired or promoted. And I certainly had no clear idea how I could improve upon my performance. It wasn't until I got my raise that I figured out my performance was acceptable.

Effective feedback paints a clear picture. It focuses on a specific situation, event, or behavior. It helps the receiver understand what's been observed or what meeting expectations "looks like." This is true for positive feedback as well. "Good job" doesn't hold much significance. I wouldn't know what aspect of my performance was good in order to repeat the performance again in the future. Telling me that producing a deliverable that only required five edits and was twenty-four hours ahead of schedule is much clearer feedback. I know what you saw and appreciated about my work, and I am likely to want to repeat or exceed this performance in the future.

It can say more about the giver than the receiver.

Many years ago, I attended a week-long course with members of my cohort graduate course. We split into small groups to work on a project. Our all-female group finished early and decided to use our downtime to provide each other with feedback about first impressions we had made on each other. My classmates told me that upon first meeting me they had hoped I'd drop out of our graduate program. They said it because I was married at the time, had my own biological son, was articulate, and had my own consulting practice. I was hurt and stunned. Until I realized that this "feedback" was less about me and more about them. There wasn't anything I could even do with the so-called feedback. What it reflected said more about them and some of the issues they were facing (being single, struggling with infertility, and having the vision of starting their own consulting practices) than anything about me. So, I gladly "hated it and spit it out." In the midst of transition fog, some of the feedback you will get is much more about the giver and their projections than it is about you. Please remember to sift through the feedback with this in mind.

It asks the receiver to accept responsibility and accountability.

Our first temptation may be to dismiss the feedback. If we refuse to believe there's something we need to change, we won't have to do anything about it. Perhaps you've gotten the results of a medical test and are advised to change your diet. But you feel just fine. Isn't it easier and tempting to continue eating as you have been despite this feedback? We often reject feedback that we don't want to have to respond to with action and accountability. It's much easier to behave the way we want under the assumption that it will be fine.

The bottom line is that we often hate feedback because most people haven't developed skills for delivering it. That means we're often on the receiving end of some poorly delivered feedback. Or we're in the uncomfortable position of providing it without knowing how to do it effectively. Poorly communicated feedback can only add to transition fog.

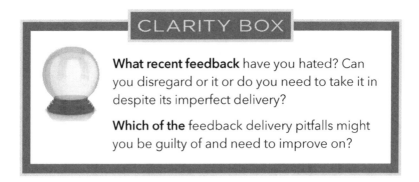

CLARITY BOX

What recent feedback have you hated? Can you disregard or it or do you need to take it in despite its imperfect delivery?

Which of the feedback delivery pitfalls might you be guilty of and need to improve on?

ADORING IT

Not all of us need the same amount of feedback as others. Some of us like to talk things out and solicit lots of feedback when we're feeling foggy. And some of us prefer to take feedback inside ourselves...

Yet, feedback can be invaluable. I can't tell you how often I hear clients try to justify that they don't give feedback freely because they themselves don't need it and feel it's overrated. But in this case the golden rule doesn't cut it. It *isn't* okay to "do unto others as you would have them do unto you." Just because you don't need much of it, doesn't mean others don't. This is where the platinum rule comes in: "do unto others as *they* would have you do unto them." Providing feedback helps others feel seen and attended to—noticed.

Our job is to deliver it in a way that maintains their self-esteem and that they can hear. The sharing of feedback delivered with candor and care is something to be adored. As Edie Seashore reminds us:

"What receivers do with feedback is totally within their control. They can reject all of it, or any part of it, swallow it whole or spit it out, distort it, *adore it*, hate it, forget it, or remember it forever."

Where does your most valued feedback come from? Who do you trust explicitly with your trials? It's critical in uncertain times to have at least one go-to person who sincerely cares about you and is willing to tell you the truth when that's what you need to hear. You need someone who can deliver it in a way that you can take it in. Or who knows when to let you work things out for yourself, but who will wait in the wings to support you.

I had just that friend in my life during a major transition. We used to take long walks each day. My mindset and mood were as variable as the weather. When she didn't want to influence me but wanted to give me space and support she'd simply say, "I want whatever you want." I've always cherished that feedback and line of unconditional support.

We underestimate the impact and power of feedback.

Leaders need feedback. By virtue of where they sit in the organization, they get removed from the realities deeper in the organization. Because they hold power, the information they get is often heavily filtered. And few people are willing to give them specific feedback about their leadership impact. Yet, real feedback can boost their effectiveness, especially during times of change. Leaders who seek feedback and demonstrate comfort with receiving it will reap the benefits.

Marriages crumble in the wake of being inattentive to our partners.

Great employees leave great organizations when they stop feeling valued. Feedback demonstrates value and manages turnover.

Our children need feedback. It communicates how much we love them.

If you ask me, those are some pretty powerful reasons for adoring feedback.

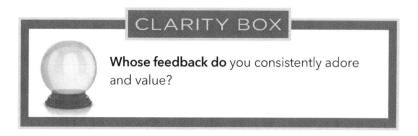

CLARITY BOX

Whose feedback do you consistently adore and value?

REMEMBERING IT FOREVER

I recently sent out an electronic newsletter to all of my business contacts. I was pleasantly surprised to hear from a past client and former marketing executive, Jim. I had worked with him eighteen years ago. Jim was successful enough to have retired at an early age, and we hadn't talked since. His email surprised me:

> "I still remember the work you did for me at our company. I consider the complete process we went through of what I would best describe as "morale improvement" as one of my most satisfying achievements as a people/team manager. And none of it would have been possible without your interviewing my staff and synthesizing their concerns, what they liked and what they didn't. You provided the necessary groundwork that we could then, together, work from."

It had been long enough ago that I couldn't recall the exact work he was referencing, although my colleague, Paula, and I had been engaged there for a few years. But I was curious, so I arranged a phone conversation with Jim. He remembered the work in great detail. One piece of it involved interviewing every member of his sizeable team. The feedback was anonymously compiled and shared with Jim as he transitioned into his new leadership role.

However, what resulted from talking to his team members was some difficult feedback that needed to be shared with one of his key managers, Carlos. As he reminisced, he admitted how tempted he was to put that feedback in a drawer rather than have a difficult talk with Carlos. He described the feedback he needed to share with his direct report as "pretty damning about him and his management style." But Jim delivered it. He recalled:

> "Carlos could have reacted with denial or outrage, but he didn't. He said 'I'm gonna fix it.' He was genuine. And his response came from the heart. Carlos went off on his own and found a career coach. He took the feedback as a positive and consciously decided to change his style. He transformed his impatient, insistent, quick-talking, shoot from the hip, no-time-for-talking style into one that became very people-minded. Carlos went on to be well regarded. He also retired early, but we've remained connected over the years. I can attest that providing that feedback was a pivotal intervention."

Jim's sharing was a real testament to the power of feedback. It began with the benefit of talking to each team member and asking for their feedback. It demonstrated the value of that feedback for Jim in his new role, and ultimately revealed a blind spot that Carlos needed to have highlighted. What moved me most though was that Jim was still talking about the impact all these years later.

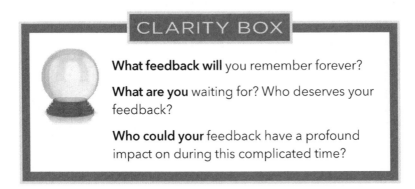

CLARITY BOX

What feedback will you remember forever?

What are you waiting for? Who deserves your feedback?

Who could your feedback have a profound impact on during this complicated time?

MASTERING PLAN "BE":

✤ Get ready. Feedback is inevitable during uncertain times.

✤ Bear in mind that most feedback is intended to be helpful.

✤ Remember, feedback is simply information. Hit the reset button when confusing feedback comes your way. Get quiet. Pay attention to your inner voice or gut. Decide for yourself what to do with it.

✤ Be open to difficult feedback that may be illuminating your blind spots and providing necessary information for you right now.

✤ Consider the source—people bring their own experiences and conditioning to their feedback, and at times it says more about them than you.

✤ Give positive feedback more freely—it will result in more positive feedback for you!

✤ Notice how gracefully some people accept feedback. Become one of them.

CHAPTER 8

BE WARY OF THE EITHER/OR TRAP

"How wonderful that we have met with a paradox.
Now we have some hope of making progress."
—NIELS BOHR

THE COMMITTEE MEMBERS were once again hunched over documents detailing the results of the corporate-wide employee engagement survey results. They had held numerous meetings focused on ways to increase employee satisfaction. I was there to advise them on the changes. We had been toiling at this for months, so focusing on actions felt like great progress.

That is, until the senior-most leader in the room exclaimed, "Good, maybe we can finally stop focusing on the employees, so we can focus on what really matters—the clients."

All of the air left the room. It seemed no one could catch his or her breath. No one uttered a syllable. The silence said it all. Did he really think the clients were most important? After all, if employees weren't satisfied, how could they create satisfied clients? But then again, the employees weren't more important than the clients either.

Without clients who were satisfied enough to keep coming back, there wouldn't be employees to think about.

So, who deserved this company's focus—the employees or the clients?

SUPPLEMENTING "OR" THINKING WITH "AND" THINKING

During uncertain times, we want answers. Enough of the gray fog; we want to see clearly. Should we focus on A or B? Should we do X or Y? Should our organization be this or that? But there aren't nice, neat, either/or solutions for all problems. Realizing that is critical. Trying to choose one option over the other may just add to your confusion.

Is it better to tell your staff what to do or ask them what to do? Should the organization be rigid or flexible about their policies? Is it better to be structured or informal? Should your organization embrace tradition or innovation? Is it better to focus on the long-term or short-term? Centralize or decentralize? Give your focus to work or home? Satisfy your boss or your significant other? I dare you to choose. You can choose one over the other, but you may see better outcomes from leveraging the benefits of both.

Trying to resolve some issues by choosing one option over the other doesn't necessarily make sense. Can you imagine having to choose between loving your oldest child OR your youngest child. To spend your money OR to save your money. These are not problems to be solved. We need to BOTH save AND spend. We love BOTH our youngest AND oldest children—and all the others in between.

It's important to realize that sometimes our uncertainty comes from trying to solve unsolvable problems. Whether to focus on employee satisfaction or client satisfaction is an unsolvable problem. We can't resolve it by choosing one over the other. It's important to pay attention to both employee satisfaction *and* client satisfaction.

During uncertainty, it serves us well to remember that not every problem requires an either/or solution. Trying to choose between one or the other will add to your stress. Your issue may be a polarity to leverage, which is all about both/and: both spending and saving, both pleasing your boss and your significant other. Choosing isn't necessary. (Whew!)

WHAT IS A POLARITY?

According to Barry Johnson, creator of the Polarity Map® and author of the books *Polarity Management* and soon-to-be published *AND*, polarities are interdependent pairs.[15] Neither is intrinsically better or worse than the other. When either/or answers aren't clear, it's because the choices may actually be polarities, where choosing isn't optimal or even sustainable over time.

Rather than explain it, let me demonstrate what a polarity is. Try this. Inhale deeply and hold it. Hold it. Hold it. Before long you'll feel uncomfortable. So...exhale slowly. Now, hold that exhale. Hold it. Hold it. How long can you wait before needing to inhale? Now, go back to your normal breathing. Notice the natural interplay between the two. Neither is favored nor deserving of more attention. It's crazy to think about debating which is better—inhaling or exhaling. Isn't it? They both have their merit, and held too long, they both have their downsides. We don't walk around trying to solve the inhaling/exhaling problem. We see it for what it is—a polarity to be leveraged—a situation in which each side has benefits and drawbacks. We accept that we need both, and that they are equally valuable. We move between the two. Leveraging them means maximizing the upside benefits of each and minimizing the downside limitations of each.

Here's an interesting and oversimplified way of applying this thinking to a common tension between tradition (the way it's been) and innovation (the way it could be) that often plays out during times of change in organizations. (see figure 1) There are many positives that result from focusing on maintaining traditions in our organizations and the core of who the organization is, like upholding our mission and values. There are also many upsides to innovation and a willingness to change with the times, like creating a competitive advantage. An overreliance on either can get us in trouble though, resulting in outcomes like stagnation or an overwhelmed staff who can't keep up with all the changes.

(Figure 1)

Positive results from focusing on the pole of **TRADITION**	*Positive* results from focusing on the pole of **INNOVATION**
* Upholds our mission and core values * Maintains practices that still serve us well * Creates stability * Upholds our historic reputation	* Can adapt to changing needs of customers * Creates competitive advantage * Leverages technical advances * Creates openness to new business arrangements
Negative results from overreliance on this pole to the neglect of the other pole	*Negative* results from overreliance on this pole to the neglect of the other pole
* Stagnation * New plans and ideas aren't seriously considered * Fall behind in the market	* Abandonment of proven processes we need * Staff can't keep up with the changes * Increased risk of error

Barry Johnson and Polarity Partnership LLC's detailed Polarity Mapping model and process (see Appendix A) takes a deeper dive on this concept and the dynamic flow of energy and interdependencies between polarities.

I once facilitated an auditing team retreat where we put this to use. The members were in conflict and needed help solving an ongoing problem. Their work required a lot of attention to detail. Some members worked slowly and diligently to ensure they were being as accurate as possible. They saw themselves as conscientious. Others on the team valued that, but were accountable to their internal clients and senior leaders for meeting deadlines and keeping the work moving. I'm sure the team members were hoping our work at the retreat would help them determine which view was right.

Obviously, neither one was right. The team needed to be BOTH conscientious AND timely. It was helpful to map out this polarity and show them the need to create a strategy that took both into account and bridged the worlds of accuracy and timeliness. For example, one strategic action was to create project plans that included completion checkpoints to keep things moving toward the final deadline and ensure timeliness. When it came to accuracy, one of their actions was to be clearer in the delegation process and to do a better job of explaining what "good enough" looked like. In other words, just how much detailed analysis needed to take place for it to be satisfactory?

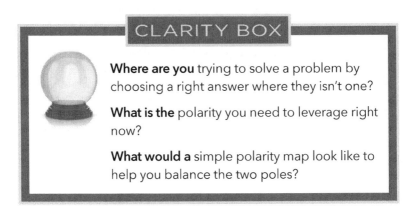

CLARITY BOX

Where are you trying to solve a problem by choosing a right answer where they isn't one?

What is the polarity you need to leverage right now?

What would a simple polarity map look like to help you balance the two poles?

THE TWO BIGGEST POLARITIES OF TRANSITION FOG

During times of stress and uncertainty, we often struggle with how to "do ourselves." We get confused between acting or reflecting, listening to our heads or listening to our hearts, and tending to our professional lives or our personal lives. If we aren't conscious about it, we may get off-balance by gravitating toward one pole without a realization of the importance of the other pole.

We see these as problems to solve and tough choices to make, when in fact they are polarities to leverage. When we stop thinking of one as better or worse than the other, or one as right and the other wrong, new possibilities open up.

1. Doing and being.

In a culture where action is highly valued, this notion of doing vs. being seems like a choice we face routinely and need to make. We know both are important, but most leaders do far better with doing then being. When we *do*, it means we are busy taking action. We're moving. It feels like progress. There are upsides. We are perceived to be in control. In the workplace, we're often evaluated and judged by what we are doing or getting done.

Being can be harder. It isn't as instinctual as doing. In bad weather, do you drive on through it for fear of wasting time and a need to get to your destination? Or do you comfortably pull over to wait for it pass? Most of us plug along, even if slowly, because pulling aside feels like a loss of progress.

A typical leader's schedule doesn't allow much time for reflecting and thinking. I can still recall the image of my calendar from my corporate leadership days. It was blocked full of meetings. What does yours look like? Taking time to *be*—whether it's to catch your breath, take lunch, or regroup—requires conscious calendar management. There is so much upside to *being*. But in my experience, leaders dealing with change and complexity tend to see it as a luxury. They tend to become lulled into a false sense of security that they are in control so long as they keep acting and getting things done.

Doing and being each have downsides if you overly rely on either. If you race to make things happen too quickly, you may miss the opportunity to consider all options and possibilities. You may make missteps. Yet, if you spend too much time reflecting and planning, you may get analysis paralysis. Then, nothing ever moves forward.

As a coach, I hear leaders' reluctance to truly leverage this polarity. Action is revered. Just *being* is scary. But the coaching sessions themselves are valuable opportunities to step back, reflect, and consider next moves. I help leaders give themselves permission *to be*—which to them can feel like a disloyal choice over doing. It's perceived as a less professional or less dedicated option. Yet, when these leaders find a way to leverage this polarity, they also find peak performance.

Years ago, a colleague retired from her job. She was faced with the tension of figuring out what to *do* next or whether she could just simply *be* retired. She wasn't sure what post-retirement would look like. So, she entertained many conversations and options about everything from employment to volunteer work to travel. After "doing" her homework, she took a long road trip with her spouse across country. That was the "being" part of her decision. She enjoyed the trip and didn't do anything but visit with family and friends, journal, and enjoy the journey. It was unusual for her to take this kind of reflection time. She was a person of action. But after taking time to think, she felt better prepared to make some big decisions and move forward.

In times of uncertainty, we feel like we have to keep moving, keep doing. No time to waste. But that expenditure of energy requires equal time to recharge and just be. Doing so will keep you fueled up and able to complete the race, which is more like a marathon than a sprint.

Here's my crazy summary. You may feel like you should know

what to *do*, but paradoxically you can't know until you *be*. Only after being can you know the action to take.

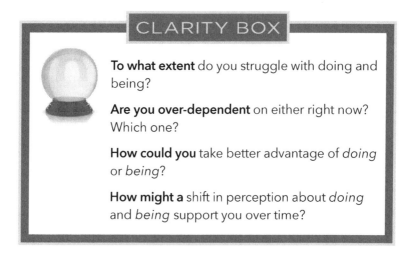

CLARITY BOX

To what extent do you struggle with doing and being?

Are you over-dependent on either right now? Which one?

How could you take better advantage of *doing* or *being*?

How might a shift in perception about *doing* and *being* support you over time?

2. Logic and emotion.

When we're in an unsettled state, we may get muddled in our decision-making. Should we listen to logic or pay attention to what our emotions and guts are telling us? Your personality style may naturally gravitate toward one of these over the other. Your gender and how you've been socialized may also play a role in over-dependence on either logic or emotions. But under the stress of a big change or decision, you may find yourself vacillating.

The key is to avoid being so logical that you don't factor in emotions—yours or others. But it's also important to avoid being so emotional that you don't make good objective decisions. Great decisions are born by weighing each appropriately—what you think as well as how you feel. We need to be sure we aren't treating this as an OR-thinking problem to solve or we could be in trouble. Using AND-thinking leverages the benefit of both our logic and emotions in these times of transition and decision-making.

Here are similar opportunities for supplementing your OR-thinking with AND-thinking.

Your head knows you should fire an employee for poor performance, but you are torn, knowing the personal impact it will have on him and his family. After all, he's not a bad guy; his performance just isn't what it needs to be.

The budget says you should consider eliminating the annual leadership retreat, but you feel torn because it would be great for morale to move ahead as planned.

You know this big promotion will be great for your career, but it means uprooting the family—again.

You're being recruited for a new position in another organization that pays more, but you know it would be hard to leave your team behind.

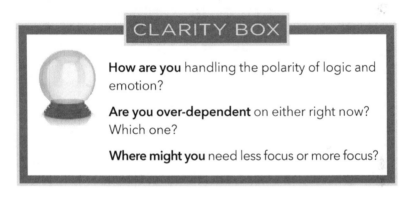

CLARITY BOX

How are you handling the polarity of logic and emotion?

Are you over-dependent on either right now? Which one?

Where might you need less focus or more focus?

When we are experiencing changes and uncertainty, it can be hard to know what to pay attention to—logic or emotion. The key is to give appropriate attention to both. Perhaps you move ahead with the annual leadership retreat to keep morale up and to provide an opportunity for these significant players to come together during this time of rapid change. But you also manage your budget by having the retreat onsite in order to save money. Or perhaps you decide to cut elsewhere in the budget to offset this important meeting. Good leaders appropriately factor in both objective and subjective data in decision-making. And they stay on the upside of each, avoiding the downsides of an over-dependence on either.

THE THORNIEST UNSOLVABLE PROBLEM

Work *or* home life—now, that's one unsolvable problem. Choosing between them can land us in trouble. But we're tempted, especially when leading big changes in the workplace. We know we need to give appropriate attention to both, but that can be easier said than done. Yet, overly focusing on one over the other can have big consequences. I've witnessed too many people pay dearly by not staying in the upsides of each of these worlds.

Focusing on work and career has many upsides: promotion potential, providing for your family, financial security, making a difference through your work, and "getting ahead." But an over-dependence on it may lead to burnout, stress, health issues, and resentment. It may mean you are making costly sacrifices in your personal life.

It's an all-too-common struggle.

I consulted to a high-tech industry during their "heyday." It was an exciting place to experience. It vibrated with energy and possibility and youth. Young, bright employees worked around the clock. These t-shirt clad employees were mostly millionaires. Whenever I talked with them, they appreciated the upsides of their situation. But they also acknowledged and lamented the trade-offs—no personal life, financial golden handcuffs that kept them there, and a youth they wouldn't get back.

In another case, I had a lunch reunion with a leader I'd known for years. I had dragged my divorcing, uncertain self to it, dreading that part of my life update. But as I finished, he look at me intently and said, "My life must look pretty perfect to you as you look at it from the outside, huh? I've climbed the corporate ladder of every firm I've been with. I've managed to remain married. And I'm financially secure. But you have something I don't: a wonderful relationship with your children. In that way, you are far richer than I am." His regret was evident. And he was working hard to refocus and repair those relationships at the time we met.

My colleague and entrepreneur extraordinaire, Louis Upkins, Jr., dedicated his book *Treat Me Like a Customer* to the topic.[16] In it, he explores how to leverage this polarity by treating those closest to you as well as you would treat your customers. As he puts it, "In most cases we don't actually choose our work over our families but rather allow it to consume us, almost by default."

Sadly, I could fill pages with examples that range from the colleague who chose a work commitment over his father's last day on earth. Or the leader who never formed friendships with his neighbors because he always knew he'd be moving away eventually and didn't have spare time for friends.

Clearly, our home lives need our attention. There are many upsides—a chance to create healthy bonds with our loved ones, time for our own self-care, the opportunity to pursue other interests, and a chance to refuel for the workplace, just to name a few. But during times of great change, complexity, and demand at work, it can be easy to sacrifice this, even unconsciously.

On the other hand, as a working professional, being overly focused on home life could be problematic. If work is always taking a backseat, you may appear to be less committed, too rigid about work hours, or inflexible about travelling. This could limit career growth and even put your job at risk if you are too distracted or overly focused on this pole.

And while I've seen fewer leaders suffer the downsides of being overly focused on their personal lives, I have witnessed personal life scenarios that have made it difficult for leaders to focus at work, perform well, advance, or keep their jobs.

The reasons have varied greatly: a child born with special needs, an ailing parent, a personal tragedy, the distraction of an extramarital affair, or greater interest in enjoying the perks of the job rather than the job itself (meaning the person does the bare minimum to collect the paycheck).

I hope you can find a way to leverage this polarity and embrace the two worlds you live in—work and home. I hope you are left with fewer regrets in either space. It sure beats wrestling one to the ground and declaring it as less worthy.

What does that look like?

I've watched several young professional parents who were struggling with travel schedules that took them away from their young children. They found some creative ways to bring a flow between their work and family lives.

One took her daughter's stuffed animal, Snowflake, with her on her travels and photographed it throughout her trip—in the conference room, on the train, and even at the beach during her downtime. She texted the pictures back home to make it fun for her daughter to see what Mom and Snowflake were up to while she was away.

Another dad travelled extensively around the globe, leaving his two daughters home with Mom. He came up with a brilliant way to help his children see his job as not something that took Daddy away from home, but as an educational opportunity instead. He began to talk with them about the diverse places his work was taking him. And together, they'd do some research on those destinations. He used that time to teach them about geography, while also helping them picture where he was. It gave them a lot to talk about when he returned, and it bridged the two worlds.

One leader I know invited his team members' personal lives into his team retreat. He asked each team member to bring an item from their childhood and talk about what it meant. He reported how impactful it was to bridge those worlds. And although it had been years since he'd done the activity, he could still recall the items his team members brought from home and the significance it held for them.

There are plenty of problems to solve during times of change and uncertainty, but work and personal lives isn't one of them. It's a *polarity* to be mindful of. Great leaders understand this, model this, remember this about their employees, and coach others about it.

Times of significant change in the workplace may require you and others to spend extra time in the office or to take more work home. Stress can be high and the normal balancing of work and family gets tipped and more pronounced during those times. Don't let the transition become the reason to over-rely on work long-term—or you'll experience the downsides of fatigue, stress, fuzzy thinking, lost relationships, resentment, and turnover.

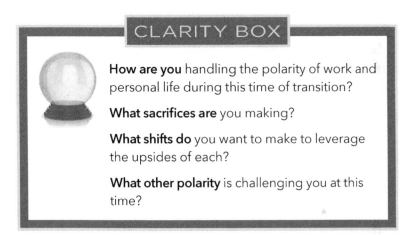

CLARITY BOX

How are you handling the polarity of work and personal life during this time of transition?

What sacrifices are you making?

What shifts do you want to make to leverage the upsides of each?

What other polarity is challenging you at this time?

MASTERING PLAN "BE"

❖ Remember that some problems are unsolvable—
   they are polarities to leverage.

❖ Catch yourself doing *either/or* thinking in situations that may be *both/and*.

❖ Review your calendar. Ensure you are making
   time to both *be* and *do*.

❖ Factor both logic and emotion into your
   decision-making.

❖ Find the flow between your work world
   and personal world. They can't be neatly
   compartmentalized.

❖ Identify unsolvable problems during this time of
   uncertainty. Help others see them for the polarities they are.

CHAPTER 9

BE FUELED BY A TBD MINDSET

"Life is like a roller coaster. It has its ups and downs.
But it's your choice to scream or enjoy the ride."
—ANONYMOUS

A SCREAMING BABY LAUNCHED a colleague of mine into a "now what?" moment that literally brought some magic into her life. Maureen started her career as a pediatric physical therapist who loved her job. But she also loved the idea of starting a family. That is, until she realized that sleep deprivation came along with being a mom. Her baby boy's startle reflex not only woke him through the night but startled the entire family out of their sound sleep as well. It put the idea of a second child completely at risk. So, this exhausted mom got desperate—and creative. She noticed how well her baby slept when cozy and secure, so she got busy sewing a sleep suit to simulate this feeling. It worked! He slept through the night. Before long, her friends were begging her for these "magic" sleep suits for their babies. And overnight (pun intended), Maureen Howard became an entrepreneur. She even went on to have more children. Her Baby Merlin's Magic Sleepsuit has made millions through word-of-mouth praise and virtually zero advertising. She now has a fulfillment center, employees, and a mission to help parents circumvent sleep deprivation and babies establish good sleep patterns.

This was never Maureen's plan. It was a "now what?" moment that she made good on. It took her from plan A as a physical therapist to plan B as an entrepreneur. For many of us, foggy times can stir up fear because things aren't going as planned. We are so convinced that plan A is the route to "success" that we panic when we're rerouted to plan B. But what if this uncertain time is showing up as an opportunity for you to reexamine how you define success? And just what if plan B reroutes you to a different kind of success? Or leads you to having an even greater impact?

The road wasn't clear or without potholes for Maureen. She admits there were many points where she could easily have thrown up her hands and turned back—through a long patent process, rejections, and feeling spread too thin at times. But she persevered. She's the proud mother of four and President of the Baby Merlin Company.

Like Maureen, the leaders I've seen deal best with transitions and uncertainty have a special way of thinking that compels them through these foggy times. They accept the situation they are in, adopt this TBD mindset, and get on the road to clarity.

By following these ten TBD mindset principles, you will also be better equipped to handle the uncertainty that has you asking "now what?" The principles are easy to understand and talk about, but much harder to carry out. How would you rate yourself? Use the box provided next to each principle to check off those that you would benefit from practicing more routinely.

☐ Feel and deal.

We all know that stuff happens. We can't stop it from happening. And when it does, we have a reaction. An emotional reaction. It's important to have that reaction, not to stuff it down. We need to express that emotion, to get it out. It's like the big exhale before we can inhale again. Or like riding a roller coaster.

When my life went sideways, I took my boys to Universal Studios in Florida. It's a theme park, chock-full of roller coasters. I was not a fan of these crazy rides, but I made it my mission to conquer them as a symbol that I could transcend fear of the unknown. The thing is, as each coaster began its upward climb, I would warn my boys that I was soon gonna scream—I mean really scream—and loudly. And I did. It was the outlet for my fear and anxiety. I had to get it out. Once I did, that scream turned to laughter, and I could enjoy the rest of the ride.

Life's uncertainties warrant some "screaming," too. How do you "let it out?" Do you talk it out, work it out in the gym, hit the driving range, or pray it out? What matters most is to *get it out*! Feel it—the anger, the frustration, the sadness. Give yourself a chance to react and do something with the emotions that may be coursing through your body, so that you can make way for clearer thinking to emerge. I'm not talking about unloading or directing your reaction at others in any unhealthy way. But I am talking about getting it out.

You may be a leader, but you're human. So, react. It's okay—at least for a short spell. Just don't get stuck in reaction mode. Simply get the emotion out of the way, so acceptance and logic can follow. Feeling it is part of dealing with it.

Others experiencing uncertainty will need time and space to react, too. As a leader at work or home, you will be in a position to support them. So deal with *your* "stuff" first, and get ready for *their* stuff to surface.

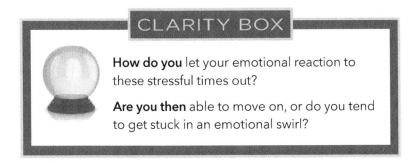

CLARITY BOX

How do you let your emotional reaction to these stressful times out?

Are you then able to move on, or do you tend to get stuck in an emotional swirl?

☐ Give yourself what you most need.

This drive through the foggy times requires fuel. In most states, the days of having an attendant fill our tanks are gone. It's all about self-serve. During these challenging times, it's all about self-service, too. Ask yourself, "What do *I* need and want right now?" And then give it to yourself. Self-care is paramount. You can wait for others to give you what you need and grow resentful when it doesn't show up. Or you can give yourself what you most need.

By taking care of yourself in this stressful time, you're managing the polarity of exertion and recovery. It can't be all about doing. Being is equally important. Being is refueling. A good way to monitor your energy expenditure is to ask yourself, "Does this action inspire me or tire me?" In uncertainty, most of what you're dealing with will drain you. So refueling is important.

What do you most need right now? To boundary your work hours? Work from home occasionally? A few laughs? A massage? To escape in a book or movie? Quiet time? To listen to some good music? Investing time in what recharges you is a worthy investment of your time. Nonstop achieving, doing, and striving has diminishing returns. So, turn your guilty-pleasures into guilt-free pleasures.

In fact, it should be guilt-free, because you owe it to others in your organization to model self-care. A leader in one organization I consulted in made it known that he left the office by 5:00 p.m. every Tuesday and Thursday to go to his spin class. It was a sacred commitment, and he made it known. Were others resentful and negative about him taking this stand? No. Quite the opposite. They respected it and even took it as permission for their own self-care. He and I were both surprised how often the positive story of him and his spin class was raised during team discussions throughout the organization.

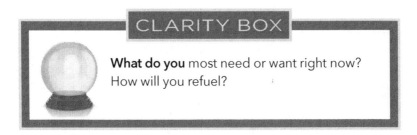

☐ Create a dream team.

You will find no shortage of people to point out all the downsides of your situation. There are well-intentioned problem solvers, cynics, and naysayers. But they will drain your energy. Your job is to surround yourself with people who believe in you and what's possible. They might be coworkers, coaches, family members, or friends. Spend more time with them instead of those who want to join in your misery.

Your "dream" team will keep you moving toward dreams that could come true on the other side of this fog. These people listen to you, boost your confidence, show unconditional support for your raggedy self, and believe in the positive outcome you have in sight.

A realtor client of mine, Liz, called recently. Having lost her husband, she scrambled to reinvent her career, finance two children through college, and face her unknown future. She relocated and went to work for a real estate team that turned out to be competitive, unsupportive, and led by a stingy boss. She wanted me to know that she had decided to "recalculate" and had recently joined another team.

Despite the challenge of trying to build a new pipeline of clients and her dwindling savings account, she was upbeat during the call. She felt confident in her transition because this new group felt like her dream team. She described a leader who was mentoring her and who believed in her. A leader who was investing in her training and making time in the evenings to check in with her to see how her showings were going. Liz's colleagues respected her knowledge and wanted to collaborate in her success. And she was benefiting from a coach who specialized in the real estate market. Liz may be in a big transition, but she's feeling buoyed by this dream team. She described them as "determined to help me succeed."

You'll know when you've found your dream team. These are people who make you forget to look at your cell phone when you're with them. And you'll feel better for having been with them. So, spend more time with them.

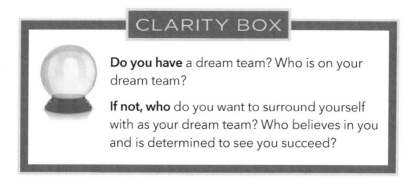

CLARITY BOX

Do you have a dream team? Who is on your dream team?

If not, who do you want to surround yourself with as your dream team? Who believes in you and is determined to see you succeed?

☐ Put the past in its place.

Don't give your past a front seat on the ride from *what was* to *what will be*. Give it a back seat. But remember that you can't safely navigate the road in front of you with your eyes glued to your rearview mirror! Resist the temptation to give your past more attention than it deserves.

Your past serves one purpose—to learn from it. Honor the past, grab the lessons, and move on. That learning will ensure that the future is even better.

If you're in a career transition, it pays to reflect on what you appreciated about your past positions as well as what you've learned that you no longer want in a job. This will help you choose a future direction. If you're being relocated for your job again, don't replay how hard that last move was, telling yourself that the family is going to freak out. Perhaps they panicked over the last move because you didn't do a good job of breaking the news to them. So, learn from that, tell yourself the family will find a way to work through this, and get on with making this transition a smooth one.

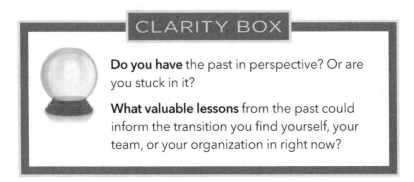

CLARITY BOX

Do you have the past in perspective? Or are you stuck in it?

What valuable lessons from the past could inform the transition you find yourself, your team, or your organization in right now?

Depending on the transition my clients are experiencing, I often use a timeline to map out some elements of their personal and professional life. This helps them to grab valuable themes and information to inform their future. With teams in transition, I do the same thing, creating what I call a graphic history map. We create a big timeline on the wall and note key elements of the past on it. It often includes when each team member joined the team, key projects over the years, notable leadership shifts and events, company locations, and so on. We then look back over the timeline to bracket and name the "chapters" of their history leading up to present day. This helps to get each team member on the same page about the journey the organization or team has been on. From there, we mine the learning from the past. We identify what no longer serves them well such that it needs to stay in the past. And we also identify what they've learned that informs the future. This activity allows the group to honor the past, grab the lessons, and strategize for the future. It always generates important dialogue. In the case of two teams I worked with who were being merged into one, it created some real lightbulb moments. With a team of physicians who were struggling to find a forward direction under new leadership, it created an opportunity to revisit a bumpy past that included the death of a dear colleague. They could then find a path forward.

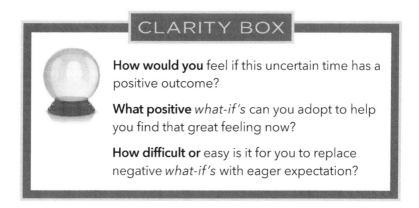

CLARITY BOX

How would you feel if this uncertain time has a positive outcome?

What positive *what-if's* can you adopt to help you find that great feeling now?

How difficult or easy is it for you to replace negative *what-if's* with eager expectation?

☐ Be joyful and positively expectant.

During uncertain times, our tendency is to focus on what we don't have and still need. That very focus cultivates fear, frustration, and an unhealthy *determination* at all costs to get what we don't have and desperately need.

We generate *what-if's* that are rooted in negatives. "What if I get fired?" "What if we lose that client?" "What if the economy tanks?" "What if the test results are unfavorable?"

But we need to take a step back and think about what we want. *Why* do we want what we want? So that we can feel good, accomplished, celebratory, confident, and secure. But the longer we focus on not having what we want yet, the longer it will take. It slows us down. And the very thing we *really* want—to feel good again—will continually outdistance us.

So, here's the real opportunity. What if you CHOOSE to feel the way you *ultimately* want to *now*? That's right. You can choose to feel good right now, even before the results show up. You can choose to think, "I don't know what it looks like, but it's going to be great!" You can convert negative *what-if's* to positive ones. "What if we get a bigger client to replace the one we lost?" "What if I love my new job better than my last job?"

When you act *as-if* the future is bright and the clarity you need is already here, you are practicing positive expectancy, and you'll be on a zip line to manifesting it.

A belief that things will be okay or even better than they were before will have you and your team acting on things from a place of can-do. It will be more likely to attract potential clients who want to work with you. It will motivate staff to want to bust out for the sake of the company rather than brush up their résumés. It will be the Petri dish that new ideas, creativity, and possibilities will grow in.

We can feel good without anything changing. It's the change of *thought* that makes a difference, not the change of *circumstances.*

☐ Be grateful for your foggy circumstances.

Fog makes us slow down. It serves a purpose. It forces us to look at what's right in front of us—right now, this moment. And only from this place of being fully present in the now can we really see all that we have to be grateful for.

Can you be grateful for the space of uncertainty you are in? At times it feels like everything is coming apart. Things at work, relationships, family, finances. Sometimes it's necessary for everything to fall away because the way things have been no longer serves us well. We're too willing to accept that things are "good enough" as they are. In order for something "even better" to take its place, some things need to dissolve.

A mid-level manager in a pharmaceutical firm tells the story of her organization. They were facing so much uncertainty in their industry. Nothing seemed predictable, and for a while there was a lot of activity that looked like scary loss. There were changes at the board level, changes in the executive ranks, unrenewed contracts, and financial concerns. These shifts had them asking "now what?" These uncertain times forced them to look at their situation and make some difficult business decisions that they had dragged their feet about for years. That included some restructuring and budget cutbacks. When I first talked to my colleague, they were in the middle of some layoffs in certain areas of the organization. Folks were feeling quite unsettled. However, those decisions and the actions that their uncertainty aroused produced one of the best business years ever for them. I ran into this same colleague while Christmas shopping at the end of that same year. She updated me. The health of the organization had resumed. In fact, they had turned a challenging year into one that produced some positive outcomes. They had even issued a bonus check to each employee at the end of the year. She was spending hers on her Christmas shopping.

I share that story because whether it's in our work lives or personal lives, what feels like crisis and crumbling is often the shedding of an old skin for a new one to take its place. Without those circumstances, we'd hobble along, satisfied that our business performance is "good enough," our mediocre relationships are "good enough," or our health is "good enough." All when they could be so much better. When things get hairy, perhaps it's time to consider the great opportunity and potential progress marked by all that is falling away. Or, as one of my favorite quotes goes, "Barn's burnt down—now I can see the moon." (Zen Master Masahide)[17]

What does your situation allow you to see differently? I have two daily practices that help me to keep perspective and stay focused on the moon rather than the missing barn.

Each morning, I used to hit the snooze alarm and begin thinking about what I "needed to" or "should" do that day. But that set my day up to be such a burden. And it certainly didn't help me feel grateful about what was to come. So, I shifted that thought to "What do I *get* to do today?" This starts my day with me thinking about what's ahead as an opportunity, honor, and privilege. It brings a different energy and mindset to my to-do list.

At the end of the day, I journal five things I'm grateful for. They are quick bullet points, and it takes me less than two minutes to do it. But it keeps my mind from obsessing on the negative aspect of the day. It excavates the good in it instead. Perhaps you've been laid off, but you're grateful for your severance package. Or perhaps you're grateful that you didn't have to initiate the ending because, if you're honest with yourself, you weren't that happy working there anyway. Believe me, I put this practice to the test when I found myself in the hospital on week twenty-eight of forty, trying not to have a scary pre-term delivery. Sometimes I had to really dig deep to find five things to be grateful for from that hospital bed, but I could always manage. You will, too.

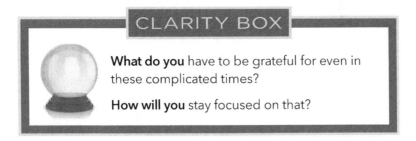

CLARITY BOX

What do you have to be grateful for even in these complicated times?

How will you stay focused on that?

☐ Be appreciative of yourself.

What does that voice in your head say *about* you and *to* you under stress? Do you know the one I'm talking about? You may recognize it by its snarky edge. We all have that inner critic in our heads. Thanks to one of my past mentors, Stephen, I've come to think of it as my "yama yama." Call yours whatever you want.

In one particularly stressful time in my life, it railed at me the whole way home from work each day. And it was a long commute. Through sixty red lights to be exact. So, it had plenty of time to berate me for what I hadn't gotten done that day. It only made my stress worse to run through my "I've still gotta..." list, never squeezing any satisfaction out of the day for what I *had* accomplished. And since there was always more to do, I was sentencing myself to a daily downer. Have you ever noticed how we count the miles left before we might be out of the fog? But what about the distance we've already travelled?

So, I made a shift. When I catch myself creating this list in my head, I now stop and begin to tick off all that I *have* accomplished that day. I run through my entire day in my head and note the accomplishments, no matter how big or small. Most days when I get to the end of that list, I think, "Damn, I'm good!" Taking stock of what I have done sheds a completely different light on the day.

I've shared this technique with many others. One night I got a text that simply said, "Damn, I AM good! This actually works!" It was from a friend who was juggling a job, schooling, and a full life. I had challenged her to try this new way of looking at each day. When she graduated, I actually found a Nike t-shirt that read, "Damn, I'm good." It was her favorite graduation gift, aside from the advice. Try it for yourself. Give yourself credit for each small step you take, and then contact me to tell me how good you remembered you are. Because you are!

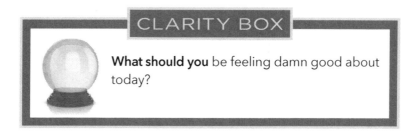

CLARITY BOX

What should you be feeling damn good about today?

☐ Be appreciative of others.

Most of us are trained as problem solvers. It's where our attention naturally goes—to what needs to be fixed, changed, and solved. And that's especially true in challenging times. But your ability to see and acknowledge what's working is what others may need most from you. They need leaders who can help them see solutions, bright spots, and progress.

In fact, recognition can be a superpower in uncertain times. It's a currency we use to show value for others. And we don't have to budget for it. We just have to remember to do it. In the course of a busy day, it's easy for all of us to forget. I caught myself years ago thinking positive things about others that I didn't share out loud—whether it was about the cashier at the grocery store, a work colleague, or one of my sons. I made an immediate "think it, say it" deal with myself. I made the commitment that if I'm thinking a good thought about someone, I'm obligated to share it. I also make it my business to share positives that I hear about others from some other source. People often share positive feedback about someone with a third party but forget to share it directly with the person who deserves to hear it.

So, catch yourself thinking positives and then figure out how to make that known. Be a leader who spreads good will and appreciation.

A client system I worked in encouraged leaders to write and send handwritten notes of appreciation to employees at their home addresses. This way the appreciation sent a ripple through the family, too. The notes often found their way back to the desks and bulletin boards in the workplace as cherished reminders.

One of my all-time favorite memories was from the children's hospital system I worked with who was onboarding new hires from across the country prior to the hospital's opening. At the end of the three-day orientation, we instructed the new hires to follow us from the auditorium to the lobby for a group picture. What they couldn't know was that around the twists and turns in the corridors, the leaders and existing staff were all lined up to welcome them aboard. All they could hear was muffled noise in the distance. When they rounded the first turn, they experienced a tunnel of smiling faces, applause, cheering, and high fives to celebrate their completion of the orientation process. When they finally got to the lobby, there was a lemonade and cookie reception for them. This became a weekly ritual during that hiring season. The cheering crowds grew each week as the previous new hires joined in to welcome others. That form of appreciation was cherished enough that when the founding CEO retired, he was surprised by a similar send-off as he navigated his last walk from his office to the parking garage. His teary reaction was caught on video.

Modeling appreciation paves the way for your team, family, and friends to do the same. It fuels a culture of positive regard in your workplace and home. No one feels they ever get enough authentic positive regard. The beauty is that when we give it freely, others want to return it to us. If you want more positive regard in your life, start sharing it with others freely.

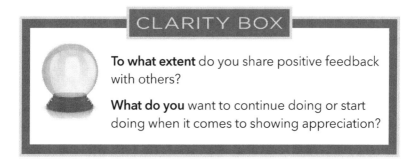

CLARITY BOX

To what extent do you share positive feedback with others?

What do you want to continue doing or start doing when it comes to showing appreciation?

☐ When it isn't fun, make it fun.

We've all used fun to make a long road trip more tolerable, haven't we? A good game of Eye Spy or the License Plate game perhaps? Well, your TBD journey will benefit from some fun, too. Fun can be another form of fuel on this foggy drive you are on. Spurts of fun are like fuel and aid in recovery at a time when we are exerting so much energy. Eighty-one percent of employees in companies that rated "great" in Fortune's list of 100 Best Companies to Work for say they work in a *fun* environment.[18] But how do you make it fun, even when times aren't feeling fun?

Here's a game I used to play with friends at the holidays. In anticipation of our respective family gatherings, we'd make up bingo cards predicting the annoying things that would be likely to happen. Grandma would buy the kids clothes in the wrong sizes again. Uncle Bob would show up at least an hour late. Aunt Mary would tell that one story for the millionth time. Then, as the day unfolded, we'd get to cross off each box as it occurred. We'd compete with our friends across town at their respective family gathering to see who got bingo first. A call or text would confirm the winner. The beauty of the game was that it transformed scenarios that would otherwise have irritated us into winning moments. It introduced some fun into the otherwise stressful time.

Today I call it Transformation Bingo. Try it. Create a bingo card about an upcoming situation you dread. Perhaps it's the complicated move your organization is making into a new building. Perhaps it's an upcoming meeting where you need to make an announcement that may not be popular. As things unfold, turn your "oh no" into "bingo."

Maureen, of the Baby Merlin Company, had to use her home as a fulfillment center for some time. She admits to being torn at times between her work demands and good parenting. She felt spread thin. So, she called "all hands on deck" when a truckload of boxes arrived at their home that had to be moved to their basement. Their family created a ramp-slide to get the boxes down the basement stairs, and the kids had great fun with it. She nostalgically recalls their laughter and the fun they made out of dismantling the boxes and feeling a part of things. In the midst of a stressful time, she used the opportunity to show her kids the importance of doing whatever it takes and making work fun.

Other clients have put on skits as parts of serious off-site retreats following a reorganization where they were trying to learn more about what each department did. Others conducted scavenger hunts through Washington, DC, as a way of encouraging greater teamwork. And others created their own version of TV gameshows to educate department members on critical new information. The bravest leader I know dressed as a rap star and made a rap video about an upcoming policy change resulting from a continuous improvement initiative.

It isn't so much *what* you do for fun during stressful times; it's more an issue of finding fun in the midst of hardship. It's about looking for some levity in trying times. It's there, but only if you look for it.

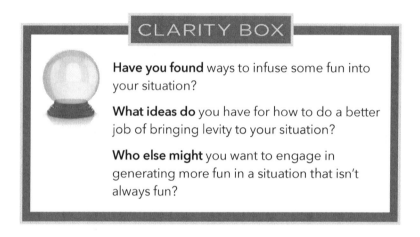

CLARITY BOX

Have you found ways to infuse some fun into your situation?

What ideas do you have for how to do a better job of bringing levity to your situation?

Who else might you want to engage in generating more fun in a situation that isn't always fun?

☐ Believe.

If you believe in whatever you're trying to make happen, you'll find the persistence you need to move through this transition. If you believe in the mission of your organization, or the product or service you have to offer your customers, it will be fuel. If you believe in the good people you work with and you believe in yourself, you will have faith. If you believe that breakdowns can be breakthroughs, you will remain optimistic. If you believe in your destination, you will have what you need to navigate this uncertainty one stretch of road at a time.

John Lennon is credited for saying, "Everything will be okay in the end. If it's not okay, it isn't the end." Can you believe that it is or will be okay, and then make it okay?

I met a fellow entrepreneur and colleague at a professional conference not too long ago. We were seated next to each other. I was drawn to Jo's kindness, easy ways, and positive energy. As we got better acquainted over time, she pieced her life story together for me. It was a journey that was pretty incredulous. She shared how she had progressed from single mom, to hair stylist and salon owner, to stylist to the A-list stars in Hollywood with an Emmy for her work. She owned candy stores, franchises, and resorts. She was what I'd consider an empire-builder. When I asked her how in the world she made this journey, her reply was straightforward: "I just never thought I couldn't. So, I did!"

Believing that you will indeed reach your destination despite the fog is more than half the battle! When fear knocks, let faith answer. Believe.

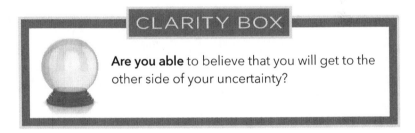

CLARITY BOX

Are you able to believe that you will get to the other side of your uncertainty?

MASTERING PLAN "BE"

❖ Give yourself permission to have an emotional reaction.

❖ Ask yourself, "What do *I* most need and want right now to stay fueled?" Give it to yourself.

❖ Create a dream team of people who will be there for you no matter what.

❖ Put the past in its place. Learn from it, but don't let it rob you of today or tomorrow.

❖ Act *as if* the best has already happened. Assume that feeling.

❖ Find reasons to be grateful for what your uncertain situation is making possible.

❖ Take inventory of how damn good you are!

❖ Use appreciation as a leadership superpower.

❖ Find the fun in not-so-fun times.

❖ Believe that what feels impossible may become inevitable.

CHAPTER 10

BE APPROPRIATELY, AUTHENTICALLY YOU

"Authenticity is a collection of choices that we have to make every day. It's about the choice to show up and be real. The choice to be honest. The choice to let our true selves be seen."
—Brené Brown

I KEPT HITTING THE snooze button on my alarm. It was that day. Weeks earlier, one of my nonprofit clients had engaged me to design and facilitate some refresher workshops on their corporate values. I agreed. And then I learned the topic: Trust. Seriously? The universe was inviting me to facilitate a workshop on trust at a time when it was sorely missing in my morphing personal life?

So, the morning of the program, I forced myself out of bed and showered. I pulled on a pair of brown pants that had always been a bit snug and found they almost fell down around my knees. I had wanted to lose that ever-evasive ten pounds, but the day was here when I had lost far more than that at the hands of stress. I stepped on the scales and burst into tears. I didn't want to lose weight like this. And I didn't feel celebratory at all. I knew I looked and felt unhealthy, yet I was just going to have to duct tape my pants on and go facilitate a workshop on trust.

Somehow I got through, but it was excruciating. I faked my way through the session, hiding my personal pain, and prayed it was the only session of its kind that I'd have to facilitate. The energy of trying to wrangle my personal situation and work assignment to stay in their places was just too much. I willed myself to believe that just maybe my personal life transition and work life would kindly keep a safe distance from each other. But that wasn't so. They just couldn't stay neatly in their own corners. So, how do these worlds appropriately coexist?

THE DREADED "HOW ARE YOU?"

Perhaps you're in that vulnerable space right now. As much as you want to keep your work life and personal lives separate, you just can't. Being unsettled in one world often affects the other.

Have you ever closed your office door to console a colleague about a personal issue? Or shared your workday stressors with loved ones around the dinner table at night? Of course.

Most of us realized a long time ago that keeping these two worlds separate, even on a good day, is darn near impossible. Now, throw in some turmoil, and forget about it! We have one life, and a ripple in one world creates a ripple in the other world. Sometimes we feel like we should be able to keep them neatly separated with mild and acceptable comingling—like bringing a paycheck home or displaying family photos safely within the confines of a wooden picture frame on your desk. But it's not that simple.

You know what I mean if you've ever found yourself cowering at the innocence of a well-intended question like "How are you?" Oh, how I've dreaded that question at times. Because I didn't know. How *was* I? Well, it was yet to be determined. Could I tell them I'd let them know in a few months? Years? Did they really want to know about my worries? Did they really care about my sleepless nights?

Should I admit to my anxiety or give them the "fine" they were used to hearing? Where should I draw the line with my sharing? Could they see I wasn't myself? How far did I let them in? Would they accept me as I was right then? All this went flashing through my head as a result of someone simply asking how I was!

It's hard to know how to show up appropriately and authentically in the midst of stressful and uncertain times. It's equally confounding to know how to show up for others who are in angst. A young professional is awaiting the results of a health test and melts down when her colleagues critique her dry run of a presentation. The newly appointed CEO suddenly finds that his newfound status is filling the gym with new runners vying for the treadmill next to him. The newly single coworker shows up alone at the office holiday party. A leader struggles to know how to show up for his staff when he learns a team member committed suicide on the heels of being laid off.

Times of transition can be confounding and lonely. But sometimes, we just can't go it alone. We need some help navigating that transition fog. We need to figure out with whom we can comfortably answer the question "how are you?"

I am so often called upon to coach leaders. It's not because of some special certification or coaching superpower bestowed on me, but instead because I bring my whole self, complete with professional expertise and life experience, appropriately to the engagement. As such, the leaders I work with feel comfortable doing the same, and that often leads to some breakthrough moments that enhance their work and home lives simultaneously. Focusing only on a client's work world with no acknowledgement of his/her personal world can be pointless. It's like blowing up a balloon that has a hole in it. Instead, knowing we have one, not two lives, we create a plan that serves both fronts.

A few years ago, I began to notice an interesting phenomenon with my coaching assignments. Organizations were hiring and paying me to coach their executives and key leaders on their work performance and to support them in their roles. But many of these same executives also wanted to hire me out of their personal coffers to work with them confidentially on the side.

Why? Because they wanted to take a deeper dive on their personal life issues. They wanted to explore their personal life purpose, work through deep nagging personal dissatisfaction, discuss future visions that could ultimately lead them out of the organization, or take a closer look at a personal trait they needed to work on. And they didn't feel that these topics were appropriate for work-sponsored coaching since they were personal in nature.

But a leader's self-proclaimed need to look at his impatient nature certainly impacts interactions at both home and work. And it's no coincidence that an executive questioning whether he should trade his stressful job for one that better suits his personal life is the same executive being scrutinized by his boss for lack of engagement. And it's no surprise that a leader whose home life is disintegrating is distracted at work. Finding clarity in one world can have a direct positive effect on the other. But we've been conditioned to think of it as more appropriate and honorable if we can keep them nicely segregated.

When our worlds bleed over, we benefit from help. Times of uncertainty tend to be lonely. No matter your title, your salary, your IQ, your last performance review status, or your ability to lift a certain amount of weight at the gym, you are not exempt from the benefits of support. That may come in the form of one person or a team of people. Perhaps it's a coach, a wise friend, a compassionate colleague, a human resources associate, a therapist, your clergy, your boss, or your partner. Your source of support may even come from unexpected people who can play that role for you. I've always been intrigued by who shows up in that capacity just when I need them.

The only prerequisites are that you can answer the "how are you?" question truthfully with them and feel supported.

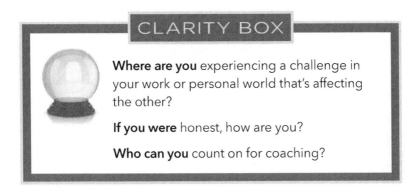

CLARITY BOX

Where are you experiencing a challenge in your work or personal world that's affecting the other?

If you were honest, how are you?

Who can you count on for coaching?

OPEN THE WINDOW

How we show up and how much we let others see becomes a choice with each interaction we have. In fact, it's yet another polarity to manage. Sharing and privacy. Letting people in or keeping them out. There is great power in authenticity, but it can be tricky. Exchanges with coworkers, friends, neighbors, family, and even random strangers in the grocery store line have us doing battle between our authentic self and the self we show the world during uncertain times.

You could think about yourself as a window. If you were a window, you might be a wide-open window with no shades. Or you could be a window protected with blackout shades that no one can see through. Perhaps you'd have adjustable shades that you could pull up or down. No matter, at night, it's likely that others would look in and see more than you know.

Let's name this window. It's the Johari Window.[19] Well, *we* aren't exactly naming it. The word "Johari" is taken from the names of Joseph Luft and Harry Ingham, the psychologists who developed the model in 1955. It is a classic, simply elegant model used to help people understand their relationship with themselves and others.

Johari Window

	Known to Self	Not Known to Self
Known to Others		
	Arena	Blind Spot
Not Known to Others		
	Façade	Unknown

(Credit to Joseph Luft,and Harry Ingham (1955). "The Johari window, a graphic model of interpersonal awareness". *Proceedings of the western training laboratory in group development*. Los Angeles: University of California, Los Angeles.)

There are four panes in the window.

The **Arena** or sometimes called **Open** pane contains information that we know about ourselves and that others do, too. This is either because it can be directly observed or has been shared by us. It's information made public. For example, you know your name and title, and so do others.

The **Façade** or **Hidden** pane contains information that we know about ourselves, but others don't know. This may be because we haven't shared the information, because it just hasn't surfaced, or because we want to keep it private. Perhaps we feel it wouldn't be appropriate to share, or perhaps we don't trust sharing this information. For example: as a leader, you don't agree with the changes going on at work but can't admit this to your team and still expect them to comply.

The **Blind** pane is just what it sounds like—a blind spot. It contains information that others know about us that we aren't aware of. It's information we can't see about ourselves, and the only way we glean it is through the feedback of others. For example, your executive presence is being questioned, but you are the last to know that you're not meeting expectations in the way you dress or behave.

The **Unknown** pane holds potential for us and others to learn more. New awareness may emerge here. These are things we nor others are currently aware of.

In each of our windows, the individual windowpanes can be of different sizes. For some of us, the Open pane is the biggest of the four. Sharing with others, being self-aware, and being receptive to feedback grows this pane. In contrast, some of us have very small-sized Open panes as a result of sharing very little, being slow to trust, and having much more information held in reserve in the Hidden pane.

At an extreme, a very large Open pane could also be indicative of oversharing and suggest that you may have some blind spots. On the other hand, under-sharing may make you feel safe and maintain an image of perfection, but it may also make you seem less real and accessible to others. That may limit the support you get from them and make them reluctant to open up to you.

During unsettled times, you may find yourself struggling with what information or feelings to share and what to withhold. It's understandable.

PITFALLS TO AVOID

Pretending to know

Many years ago, I received a call from my friend Brad who had just started a big new job. His strained voice recounted the details of his first team meeting. He painted the picture of sitting at the head of the conference room table, excited to be there, when a direct report asked him a difficult question. It was a question he didn't really know the answer to, so he faked an answer. I asked why he didn't simply say, "I don't know." He admitted that it didn't occur to him in that moment to be so authentically honest as to admit he didn't know something. In hindsight, he realized it would have been the best response. But in his mind, "I don't know" wasn't something leaders said. His quick attempt to fake an answer undermined any credibility he needed to build with his team, and he just couldn't get it back. He and his employer parted ways in short order.

It was a costly lesson for him and one you can avoid. When you're moving through any type of transition fog, there will be a lot that you can't see or know. Find the power of "I don't know." Bring what you don't know into the open. This authentic admission garners respect and trust.

Compartmentalizing and role playing

Do you worry what would happen if people saw the "real" you at work? More importantly, have you considered the consequences of them *not* seeing a "real" you at work? I've seen many leaders struggle with this dilemma of how *to be* in uncertain times, as well as how to reconcile their work personae with their home personae. So, they compartmentalize. They not only separate the two lives but *who they are* in each life. They begin to behave the way they think they "should" and end up playing a role, whether they realize it or not. They behave the way they think a leader, parent, pastor, (fill in the blank) "should." In the process, they are unrelatable. Others can't connect to them. And a sort of suspicion arises. Who are they really?

My colleague shared this story from his own consulting practice. One of his clients was a leader who was experiencing a big uncertainty in her personal life, having been diagnosed with a serious medical issue. Let's call her Kathy. She barely skipped a beat and avoided talking about it altogether at work, although everyone knew about it. And while on one hand she was lauded for her courage, strength, and dedication, her team members were also a bit perplexed by the unreal response to the challenge she faced. It became the elephant in the room. They were left wondering what would be expected of them if they had a health issue. Plowing through it? Pretending it didn't happen? Working instead of recovering? It became cause for concern.

Kathy was prone to saying things like "Now, remember, I'm wearing my executive hat" before responding to something. She would announce that she was in role. The team was unsure what to make of this separation of authentic self and leadership self. As a result, her followers did as you might expect. They followed her lead. They also "played the role" of direct report in her presence, never feeling very safe to be their authentic selves, express authentic opinions, or reveal more than necessary about life outside of work. This spilled over to the team culture. They were equally reluctant to have the real conversations they needed to have as a team, to reveal challenges they faced, or to ask for assistance from fellow team members. They struggled with forming a cohesive team, opting to keep their interactions safe and transactional. My colleague found it difficult to make inroads with this client because authenticity was a barrier.

Playing a role and behaving the way we think we "should" can come at a cost. There can be unintended consequences. A simple acknowledgement of transitions we are facing at work or outside of work might be in order.

Oversharing

Sharing information in times of transition can be beneficial. However, overdone, it's a weakness. How much to share requires careful consideration. What's the impact of sharing this information, sharing it now, and sharing it with this person or group?

We may be tempted to want to get things off our chest, to share the burden, to keep people informed, and to be real. But not all information is intended to be moved into the open. When we share everything, we may be oversharing. There are times to appropriately keep information to yourself. For example, don't vent your frustration about one of your direct reports to another direct report. Or perhaps you shouldn't share detailed information about your workplace insanity with everyone at the school fundraiser dinner table.

It makes people uncomfortable, may reflect negatively on you, and may complicate an already complicated scenario. It happens. I once sat next to a new leader who was having dinner with his team as part of his transition. He was working hard to fit in and be one of the gang. When he began to share stories about his drinking and drugging days in college, he crossed the line into oversharing. And my foot found his for a quick kick under the table to dial it in.

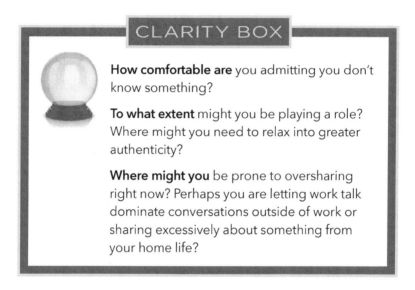

CLARITY BOX

How comfortable are you admitting you don't know something?

To what extent might you be playing a role? Where might you need to relax into greater authenticity?

Where might you be prone to oversharing right now? Perhaps you are letting work talk dominate conversations outside of work or sharing excessively about something from your home life?

BEING AN EXAMPLE TO OTHERS

Figuring out how to be appropriately authentic when you feel so exposed is no easy feat. I faced this firsthand when my consulting client became my employer. People who had known me as a consultant for many years became coworkers. I was asked routinely about my new-to-the-organization employee status. I wasn't sure what to say, so I chose to tell the truth. I explained that my life had "taken an unexpected turn, along with the economy, and this felt like the right next move." And the strangest thing happened. Being appropriately authentic and weaving some of my personal stories and realizations into my workshops, coaching, and consultations became valuable.

Living my own uncertainties helped me be more compassionate and tuned in with others. It became an unexpected gift that you may experience, too.

Here are some other examples of appropriate authenticity that worked:

* I partnered with leaders of a start-up operation who were preparing to introduce themselves to their newly formed teams in a retreat. We decided to do it in a rather unique way. The leaders didn't focus on their credentials and past work experiences so much. They told their stories. The stories of where they came from, who they were, who their mentors had been, what their greatest failures had been, and what they had learned from them. It was fascinating to watch the impact of a well-dressed, highly articulate and bright leader tell the story of growing up extremely poor in the projects with rats scampering around her bedroom. We heard her speak from the heart about her values and why she was motivated to want to serve children with challenges. The team got a fuller view of who this leader was, beyond what she had achieved and who she appeared to be. She brought down a hierarchical barrier from the start. She met people with her humanity. That was the culture the organization was striving to create.

* On a smaller scale, a coaching client confessed to me that her daughter was sick, and she was waiting for a call from her husband after they saw the doctor. She told her team that her phone was out and on the table awaiting an update, a move that was otherwise taboo in the culture. She then stepped out of the room when the call came in. She shared the story with me as an admission of her

inappropriateness in letting her personal world encroach on the work world. She broke meeting norms. She was surprised when I supported her decision. I felt that as a leader, she was appropriately prioritizing a personal need and paving the way for others to make such choices more comfortably, too.

Your team members will follow your lead. Bringing your authentic self to work when you're experiencing some issue at home or work gives them permission to do the same.

LETTING YOUR RAGGEDY SELF SHINE THROUGH

When we move information that was formerly "hidden" in the Johari Window into the "open," some amazing things can result. Your authenticity, openness, vulnerability, and risk-taking can yield interesting outcomes.

Neal was a VP hoping to continue to rise in his financial services organization. Neal was bright and articulate. He carried his schedule for the day neatly folded in his shirt pocket and was always adequately prepared. His office was immaculate and his desk rarely hosted more than one file folder on it. He focused on one thing at a time. There was simply no room for messiness in his work world. I mean, even the hairs on his head knew to disappear over time, leaving his neat, shiny scalp behind. No worries about a hair ever being out of place. He was nicely compartmentalized. So was his life and personality. Until a pivotal leadership retreat.

The senior leadership team that Neal was a part of had made a commitment to convene routinely over the course of the calendar year. They wanted to build trust, create a more cohesive team, and focus on their own development. Looking back, the CEO must have made that decision with great clairvoyance, because the following year was fraught with complexity and these sessions set this team up to face them better together. They were often chomping at the bit to focus on tasks, yet their real progress was in their discussions. As each retreat dawned, the trust in the room grew. So much so, that as facilitator, I was stunned by an accidental breakthrough for the team.

As part of a discussion on conflict, I posed some rhetorical questions as a segue to some content: "What did conflict in your family of origin look like? How does it influence how you view conflict or *engage in* conflict as a leader today?" Before I knew it, each member began to respond with great candor. They revealed information about parental expectations, family addictions, being bullied, and other personal details. The stories were from the heart and gushed from some unseen fountain inside of them that became a breakthrough for the team's development. It was information they had never heard from each other before, despite the decades some of them had worked together.

I later interviewed the CEO of this team. He revisited this scene and recalled it as one of the high points he's had working with the team. He reflected on the team dinner held at the home of one of the team members the evening of the retreat. "It was fascinating to me to see the teamwork on display, the collegiality, the comfortable and relaxed atmosphere. So, the real change was immediately evident right then."

Neal was one of the early contributors in that discussion. And he set the stage for some deep sharing. It's as though his blue jeans and casual retreat attire couldn't contain the personal Neal the same way his pressed dress shirts did. He shared his imperfect upbringing with the entire room. But it didn't stop there. In the retreat that followed months later, Neal shared an uncommon edgy and humorous comment with the team. They looked at him with raised eyebrows. Neal replied, "Oh, you wouldn't recognize me at home. I swear like a sailor and have a wicked sense of humor." The group was puzzled. There were two Neils? They kind of liked this imperfect, fun guy who showed up that day. In fact, a candid discussion ensued where they urged Neal to bring more of his authentic self to work. I told them I call it my "raggedy" self. And the term stuck.

Neal rather liked the idea of integrating his work and home self. His body language relaxed as he felt permission to be seen and accepted in ways he never thought possible. He could act less like a VP and be more of who he really was.

Weeks later, one of Neal's direct reports stopped me in the hallway. He said he knew I was working with the leadership team and wondered what I had done to them. When I probed what he meant, he said, "My boss is different. In fact, he used to drive me crazy micromanaging us. I just couldn't connect with the guy. But I really like the guy I see lately. In fact, he came to us asking for budget cuts recently, and in the past I'd have railed against him. But I found myself feeling empathic and wanting to do anything I could to help him succeed."

Neal still teases about being a more raggedy version of himself. But, he *was* recently promoted!

What would happen if you showed your raggedy self to the world? What's your worst fear? What if you discovered, much like Neal, that others would gladly accept you just as you are at this time, even if a bit raggedy from whatever uncertainties may have rocked your world? It's been my experience and observation that exposing yourself can open the door for support to flow your way. You aren't seen as weak, but rather as brave and strong in your vulnerability. In fact, your vulnerability grants permission to others to share their authentic raggedy selves.

Unless you get comfortable with your own vulnerability, it will be a continual roadblock to authenticity. How are you doing? Where might you be ready to open the blinds of that window of yours?

Here are some assumptions you may be making that you need to challenge on your way to being your authentic self in this uncertain time.

* I will be held in lower esteem if I share openly.

* I can't be respected unless I'm perfect.

* They will judge me negatively if my work and personal worlds overlap.

* They won't accept me as I am.

* They probably won't be real with me, so it feels unsafe to be real with them.

* There is one right way for leaders to behave.

* I can't share updates until I know everything and have the answers.

So often it isn't what others will think that's in the way. It's how you are thinking about and judging yourself.

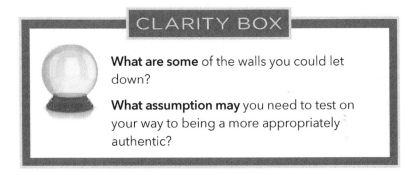

CLARITY BOX

What are some of the walls you could let down?

What assumption may you need to test on your way to being a more appropriately authentic?

HELPING OTHERS SHOW UP AUTHENTICALLY

Clearly, we can't leave our feelings behind when we leave the house in the morning, and we can't even lock them in the car in the parking garage. Nor can your team members and coworkers who are experiencing transitions and uncertainty outside of the workplace. No matter how much we wish they didn't, our feelings and issues come with us. So, what do you do as a leader when you see others struggling with this crisscrossing of worlds?

I recently did some work for a consulting client organization. The CEO was discussing how much his young leaders struggled with knowing how to deal with personal issues that followed their team members and direct reports to work. He shared that one of the twenty-year-olds on his staff had quite suddenly lost his mom. The CEO saw him in the break room early in the morning on one of his first days back from his bereavement leave. He pulled up a chair and shared that he too had lost his mom when he was young. He spent time acknowledging this big transition in the young man's life. What the CEO shared with me was his disappointment that no other leader had known how to approach this young man aside from muttering, "Sorry to hear about your mom," and then getting right down to business.

The CEO wanted to give this young man permission to *be* however he needed to be during this adjustment. He made it okay to show up as his raggedy self. When these worlds bumped into each other, his leaders froze with discomfort. What could they say? What could they do?

We talked about the downside of the well-intended "I'm here for whatever you need." It puts the ball in the court of the person already shouldering a lot. Instead, the CEO offered, "I grab coffee each morning in the cafeteria. Stop by one day this week. I'll be there for you."

New leaders are often surprised at how much personal issues show up on the job. It often gets categorized as babysitting. In truth, many leaders wish this part of the job would evaporate. But employees see it as a part of a leader's job—to demonstrate understanding and compassion. Leaders don't have to take the problems on, but they can provide an acknowledgement for those going through some rough times, rather than locking them into pretending.

Leaders with this capacity can change lives.

It literally saved my colleague's life. Cindy was a bright, amazing, put-together woman when I met her. But one day, she shared her history with me. Her life plan A didn't work out for her, and she found herself a single mom with sole custody of her three children—aged five years, two years, and three months. The baby also had special needs. Her extended family was not in the picture. She had no college degree, no means of financial support, and no plan for how to move forward. Talk about fog! She showed up at a job interview with some men she had a previous work connection with. And she brought her authentic self with her. They understood her life situation and employed her. Well, they actually did far more than employ her!

They gave her the flexibility she needed to attend her children's extracurricular events and permission to bring the children to work when in a pinch. They helped her work out a plan for pursuing a college education. When she looks back on that time, she says, "I don't know how I did it, but I dug deep. At that time, the men in my life *were* my two bosses. I worked for them for twelve years, and we are in contact to this day. One of them is in his eighties and visits each year. Both of them attended my daughters' weddings. I would have done anything for them!"

Cindy went on to hold a lofty position as a global human resources executive in a pharma organization. She credits the ability to be her authentic self and the leaders who understood that home life and work life couldn't be neatly compartmentalized. She says this was a saving grace in her life.

Happily marrying our worlds in an authentic and appropriate way isn't necessarily easy, and I won't begin to try to prescribe how and what you should do. Each situation can be so very unique. When you're having a health challenge, how do you handle that in the workplace? When you've lost your job, how do you show up at the neighborhood dinner party? When do we bring the walls down, and just how far do we go?

While there is no one way to do so, I will nonetheless challenge you to remember that our work and personal worlds are a polarity to manage.

Our job is to remember that one affects the other. You need to find a healthy flow between the two. It's like moving between two adjoining hotel rooms without changing who you are when in each room.

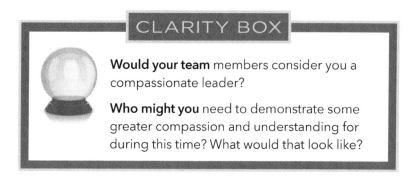

CLARITY BOX

Would your team members consider you a compassionate leader?

Who might you need to demonstrate some greater compassion and understanding for during this time? What would that look like?

MASTERING PLAN "BE"

❖ Accept it–work and personal lives can't help but crisscross.

❖ Avoid playing a role–others know you are pretending and it doesn't serve anyone.

❖ Consider any walls you would benefit from bringing down with others–your children, friends, family, coworkers. Who would you like to "let in" on what?

❖ Refrain from oversharing information.

❖ Be willing to be raggedy more often on the road to being appropriately authentic.

❖ Make it safe for others to bring more of their authentic selves to their interactions with you.

SOME FINAL THOUGHTS

I T'S DONE! OR is it? Are we ever really done with uncertainty? After all, we're born into uncertainty, live from one uncertain moment to the next, and ultimately leave the world wondering *"now what?"*

Even as you're reading about uncertainty and I'm writing about uncertainty, new uncertainties are emerging in the workplace and on the home front. If you're conjuring up an image of whack-a-mole, you're getting the gist of what I'm saying.

For me, I face an empty nest in just a few short months and I'm launching my other baby—*TBD*—into the world simultaneously. What happens next is unknown. So, I will join you in the space of transition and not knowing. Let's practice the principles I've written about here. I trust the information, conversation, and inspiration I've shared will help you transform your fears into confidence—confidence born of a knowing that we have a choice in how we navigate our foggy paths and that clarity is within reach. So, let's choose wisely, knowing that we need equal parts *determination* and *being* to reach the positive outcomes ahead.

ENDNOTES

1. Ken Blanchard, "Mastering the Art of Change," *Trainingjournal.com* (2010): Accessed July 28, 2017. http://marcishepard.org/policy/9%20Mastering%20the%20Art%20of%20Change.pdf.

2. William Bridges with Susan Bridges, *Managing Transitions: Making the Most of Change*, (Philadelphia: Da Capo Lifelong Books, Philadelphia Press, 2017), 1-2.

3. Initially described as "Four Stages for Learning Any New Skill", the theory was developed at Gordon Training International by its employee Noel Burch in the 1970's.

4. James Wooten, *We Are All the Same* (New York: Penguin, 2004).

5. "America's Most Challenging High Schools," The Washington Post, last modified May 5, 2017, https://www.washingtonpost.com/graphics/local/high-school-challenge-2017/

6. Barry Oshry, *Seeing Systems: Unlocking the Mysteries of Organizational Life* (San Francisco: Berrett-Koehler, 2007), 56.

7. Ibid.,55.

8. Peter Senge et al., *The Fifth Discipline Fieldbook: Strategies and Tools for Building a Learning Organization* (New York: Doubleday, 1994), 242-246. Note: The Ladder of Inference was first put forward by organizational psychologist Chris Argyris and used by Peter Senge in *The Fifth Disciple: The Art and Practice of the Learning Organization*, p. 243, The Crown Publishing Group, 1994. The model is used with permission by Rick Ross and Charlotte Roberts. The "reflexive loop" was first published in William Isaac's 1992 working paper, *The Ladder of Inference*, published by the MIT Center for Organizational Learning.

9. "Cognitive Reframing," Wikipedia. Accessed July 28, 2017. https://en.wikipedia.org/wiki/Cognitive_reframing

10. Daniel Goleman, *A Force for Good* (New York: Bantam Books, 2015).

11. Michael Durst, *Napkin Notes on the Art of Living* (Responsible Life Foundation, 2010).

12. Susan Jeffers, *Embracing Uncertainty*, (New York: St. Martin's Press, 2003), 267.

13. Charles N. Seashore, Edith Whitfield Seashore, and Gerald M. Weinberg, *What Did You Say? The Art of Giving and Receiving Feedback* (Columbia, MD: Bingham House Books, 1996).

14. Ibid. 53

15. Barry Johnson, *Polarity Management: Identifying and Managing Unsolvable Problems* (Amherst, MA: HRD Press, 2014).

16. Louis Upkins, *Treat Me Like a Customer: Using Lessons from Work to Succeed in Life* (Grand Rapids, MI: Zondervan, 2009). 48

17. David Schiller, *The Little Zen Companion* (New York: Workman Publishing, 1994), 147.

18. "100 Best Places to Work For" last modified March 9, 2017, http://fortune.com/best-companies/ 21 Joseph Luft, *Of Human Interaction.* (Palo Alto, California: National Press). 177.

19. Joseph Luft,and Harry Ingham (1955). "The Johari window, a graphic model of interpersonal awareness". *Proceedings of the western training laboratory in group development.* Los Angeles: University of California, Los Angeles.

APPENDIX A: POLARITY MAP

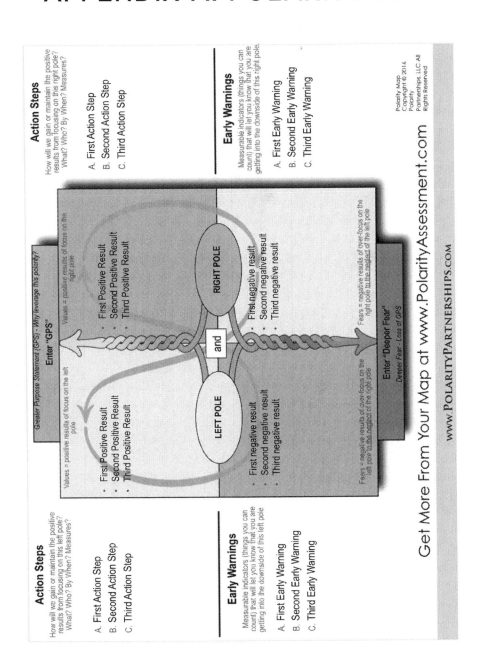

Action Steps

How will we gain or maintain the positive results from focusing on this left pole? What? Who? By When? Measures?

A. First Action Step

B. Second Action Step

C. Third Action Step

Early Warnings

Measurable indicators (things you can count) that will let you know that you are getting into the downside of this left pole

A. First Early Warning

B. Second Early Warning

C. Third Early Warning

Action Steps

How will we gain or maintain the positive results from focusing on this right pole? What? Who? By When? Measures?

A. First Action Step

B. Second Action Step

C. Third Action Step

Early Warnings

Measurable indicators (things you can count) that will let you know that you are getting into the downside of this right pole.

A. First Early Warning

B. Second Early Warning

C. Third Early Warning

Greater Purpose Statement (GPS) - Why leverage this polarity?

Enter "GPS"

Values = positive results of focus on the left pole

- First Positive Result
- Second Positive Result
- Third Positive Result

Values = positive results of focus on the right pole

- First Positive Result
- Second Positive Result
- Third Positive Result

LEFT POLE   and   **RIGHT POLE**

- First negative result
- Second negative result
- Third negative result

- First negative result
- Second negative result
- Third negative result

Fears = negative results of over-focus on the left pole to the neglect of the right pole

Fears = negative results of over-focus on the right pole to the neglect of the left pole

Enter "Deeper Fear"

Deeper Fear - Loss of GPS

Get More From Your Map at www.PolarityAssessment.com

www.POLARITYPARTNERSHIPS.COM

ACKNOWLEDGMENTS

"Alone we can do so little; together we can do so much."
—HELEN KELLER

WHEN IT CAME to writing a book, I had a vision but no sight line. Ideas but no map. Lots of uncertainty. No clarity.

I was blessed by so many who lit the way and knew the "next right thing" I needed to do. This is my attempt to remember all of you and finish before the music starts playing, and they drag me out of this book once and for all.

It all started in second grade when I promised Mrs. Wolfe I'd write a book — and that commitment haunted me forever. Mrs. Wolfe frowned on girls wearing dresses and students drinking chocolate milk, but she was always willing to cheer on a lover of books like me. I have to think she's smiling as I bring this to completion, and yes, I hear her urging me to write another one. I thank her for believing in me way back when.

My serious conversations about actually writing a book took place with Steve Harrison and his Quantum Leap team. I was in one big fog as we tossed around concepts, ideas, titles, and writing samples. Steve, Martha Bullen, Geoffrey Berwind, Deb Englander, Mary

Guiseffe, and Joe Mc Allister: thank you for hanging out in the fog with me and for all of your patience and support.

A shout-out to my 40 colleagues from our Philadelphia Oshry Worldwide Gathering who saw the title of this book more clearly than I did. The group epiphany is a memory I cherish and smile about each time **TBD** is mentioned.

Thank you Laura Duffy for turning that title into a cover. And for ignoring every idea I had in exchange for something much better.

Then there's the Station Square Media gang, led by Diane O'Connell, publishing guide, editor, and guardian angel of the process. Every time I asked *"now what?"* she provided the answer and support with the perfect blend of directness and gentleness for this new writer. Yes, Diane, I might even do this again. Special thanks to Steve Plummer, interior designer who magically turned my Word document into a real book, and to Linda H. Dolan, copyeditor, for her attention to detail and for taming my boldface and exclamation overuse! Janet, I appreciate your patience in the production process. You all brought me clarity and confidence in this process.

Deep appreciation goes out to every theorist, colleague, and author who so generously provided me not only with permission to highlight your work, but did it with such a generous spirit and humbling positive feedback. We are forever connected now.

To every client organization, leader, team or individual who has crossed my path and provided the rich content for this book. While I've done my best to keep you anonymous on these pages, I know who you are and have been fortunate to work with you.

For everyone who asked, "How's the book coming?" and unwittingly held me accountable on the journey. Or bravely asked for a copy of the manuscript and slogged through a very long and raggedy Word document in an amazing show of support. Bless you.

To my trusted assistant, Tina Liskey. Where do I begin? Thank you for being by my side on this journey. You are heaven-sent.

To the friends and extended family that I've had to put on hold at times to keep moving this work forward. Thank you for understanding, for nudging me, cheering me on, encouraging me, and weighing in on all sorts of decisions along the way with loving candor. You are the same people who have stood by my side during my life-going-sideways, uncertain times. I love you for that.

My extraordinary sons, Tyler and Jason, thank you for being my partners in uncertainty and life teachers. You make me proud. Aside from your pre-term births, you've been the easiest part of my life and the one thing I am certain of—that I will always love you. You are the fuel behind everything I do. Thank you for being you and for understanding my compulsive focus on making this happen. (And for not visibly rolling your eyes in plain view of me as I chase my dreams.)

Finally, I feel like I really need to acknowledge anyone who's reading this page. Thank you for purchasing *TBD* and reading it to the very end. May it provide you with a lens for the clarity you are seeking and confidence for the inevitable uncertainties to come. I'm always here for you.

INDEX

BRENDA K. REYNOLDS

ARE YOU LOOKING for some clarity for your organization, leadership, team, or self?

Would you like Brenda to speak at your event?

To connect with Brenda, visit www.bkrconsult.com.

Brenda is a sought-after business and change management consultant, coach, and facilitator who has advised hundreds of major corporations, nonprofits and organizations for over 20 years on how to manage the people side of change.

As an inspiring change agent, Brenda draws on her extensive consulting and personal experiences to equip individuals and organizations with easy-to-apply strategies for navigating through and managing complex transitions. Brenda's passion is helping others turn their "now what?" into a "why not!"

Brenda is also the creator of the *"Now What?" Transformation*™ *Clarity Card Deck*, a tool for anyone wanting to move through a life or business transition meaningfully, mindfully, and positively.

Brenda holds a Masters degree in Organization Development from American University and a bachelor's degree in Secondary Education and Communication. However, her most significant degree is in life experience — where she's learned from teaching 8th and 9th graders, moving from a small town to the suburbs of Philadelphia, holding two corporate leadership roles, making it through two scary pre-term labors, being an entrepreneur, single parenting, embracing life after it went sideways, doing mission work in South Africa, and guiding others who are dealing with work and life uncertainties.

Brenda is a frequent radio guest, Vistage presenter, TEDx and keynote speaker.

She currently lives in the Philadelphia area.

Her clients and her two grown sons and are living proof that amazing things can result from uncertain times.